SCHOOL LIBRARIANSHIP SERIES

Edited by Diane de Cordova Biesel

1. *Reference Work in School Library Media Centers: A Book of Case Studies*, by Amy G. Job and MaryKay Schnare, 1996.
2. *The School Library Media Specialist as Manager: A Book of Case Studies*, by Amy G. Job and MaryKay Schnare, 1997.
3. *Forecasting the Future: School Media Programs in an Age of Change,* by Kieth C. Wright and Judith F. Davie, 1999.
4. *Now What Do I Do? Things They Never Taught in Library School,* by Amy G. Job and Mary Kay Schnare, 2001.
5. *Strategic Planning for School Library Media Centers*, by Mary Frances Zilonis, Carolyn Markuson, and Mary Beth Fincke, 2002.

School Librarianship Series

The works in the School Librarianship Series are directed toward the library school professor, the library school student, and the district supervisor. Each volume examines the role of the school library media specialist as an agent of change within the educational system, with the goal of exploring the philosophical basis of school librarianship yesterday, today, and tomorrow.

Site-based management, the challenges of technology, and multiculturalism are a few of the current educational issues presented in *The School Library Media Specialist as Manager: A Book of Case Studies*. The authors present realistic situations, and thought-provoking questions at the end of each case study engage the reader in a search for possible solutions to the problems presented.

Diane de Cordova Biesel
Series Editor

Strategic Planning for
School Library Media Centers

Mary Frances Zilonis
Carolyn Markuson
Mary Beth Fincke

School Librarianship Series, No. 5

The Scarecrow Press, Inc.
Lanham, Maryland, and Oxford
2002

SCARECROW PRESS, INC.

Published in the United States of America
by Scarecrow Press, Inc.
A Member of the Rowman & Littlefield Publishing Group
4720 Boston Way, Lanham, Maryland 20706
www.scarecrowpress.com

PO Box 317
Oxford
OX2 9RU, UK

ISBN 0-8108-4104-5 (pbk. : alk. paper)

CONTENTS

PLANNING TEMPLATES

PREFACE

After the establishment of regional library systems within our state, school library media centers were requested to initiate a planning process. This had been made a requirement for grant funding through the regional and state library agencies. We quickly recognized that schools did not have the support systems of public, academic, or special libraries and would need to make the planning process as simple as possible.

The resulting project had two major objectives:

1. To provide a workbook for school library media specialists to assist them in the development of a long-range plan that would meet the requirements of the state agency.

2. To prepare a training process for regional library staff or district personnel to use in assisting individual or groups of schools in the development of a long-range school library media center plan.

The organization of this manual was developed in conjunction with the help of numerous focus groups of school library media specialists, school administrators, technology teachers/coordinators, and other interested parties. They provided the field input and ultimately validated much of the information gathered from state standards, national standards, and regional guidelines. Surveys were used to gather information on format and priorities from relevant state associations.

*We are indebted to Rubin and Himmel and Wiggins and McTighe for substantial ideas for developing the template and to the Massachusetts Board of Library Commissioners who funded the original work through an LSTA grant.

Manual Organization

The manual is organized into informational chapters that correspond with standard requirements for planning. Planning templates are included in the chapters to which they pertain. You may want to photocopy these work forms and distribute them as a packet or individually to appropriate committee members. The appendix contains three important support documents: a New England Educational Media Association (NEEMA) report on school library media competencies, a summary set of work pages, and a tip sheet for survey construction.

> *For a sailor without a destination there is no favorable wind.*

INTRODUCTION

Why Plan? Planning is a process having to do with determining:

- where you want to go
- where you are now
- ways to get from *now* to *then*

All anchored in terms of your program of services and how it contributes to student learning.

Benefits and Characteristics of Planning

- Explains your program to others
- Identifies priorities, strengths, and weaknesses
- Provides an anchor for developing a budget
- Articulates connections with school's mission
- Provides a blueprint for future development
- Creates a clear sense of purpose
- Provides for ongoing evaluation
- Provides a basis for decision making
- Provides a basis for developing accreditation documents or reports
- Provides a foundation for grant writing
- Provides a process for accountability

Who Should Plan?

Long-range planning for library media center programs is always a sound strategy, and anyone with the resources to develop a plan *should do so.*

A variety of settings may meet your particular needs:

- **School districts.** A district's comprehensive plan examines the district as a whole and indicates implementation by individual schools.
- **Individual schools (public or private)** may develop individual planning documents or choose to develop a comprehensive plan if there is more than one library media center.
- **Groups of schools within a district or region** may wish to develop a plan with each one having its own individual action plan while addressing the common needs of all.

Planning requires time and commitment—for most it is a three- to six-month effort.

PLANNING—WHAT IS IT?

Planning is a process having to do with determining where you want to go, where you are now, and ways to get from here to there. Effective planning enables you to make decisions about the key components of your practice. It helps you articulate your vision and the process of identifying the steps you need to take to be able to arrive at your vision. This guide will help in developing both *strategic* and *operational* plans. The **strategic** plan establishes a fundamental organizational tone, defines the program's business and informs staff members why they are doing what they do. The **operational** plan, on the other hand, is a more detailed account of specific organizational goals, often described on a year-to-year basis, with key activities identifying what will be done to meet the goals, by whom, and in what staffing configurations. Operational plans generate program output statements. These "outputs" describe what conditions will exist at some determined future point as a result of the implementation of the operational plan (LeBaron and Markuson, 1991). In order for one to be successful in implementing an operational plan, often called an *action* plan, you need to involve as many people as possible who will be affected by the plan in the planning process.

> **Both *strategic* and *operational* plans are essential.**

The purpose of the long-range plan is to provide an opportunity to conceptualize and describe the significant goals you wish to achieve in your school library media program within the next one to five years and to plan how to achieve these goals.

As with the development of the school district's technology plan, the school library media center plan provides a system-wide framework for the program. Individual school libraries within a given district or a private school with multiple libraries may find they need to add brief additional information that will identify particular characteristics and/or position them at a particular stage in the strategic plan. In other words, the action plan for an individual school will flow from the strategic plan, but the priorities may be different for individual libraries.

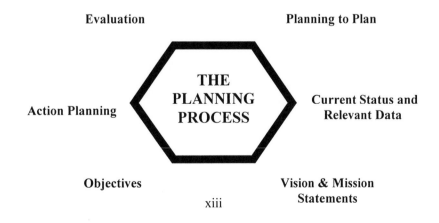

Planning to Plan

- Getting approval to do it
- Forming a committee
- Setting tasks and guidelines
- Establishing a timetable
- Developing a communication strategy

Current Status

- What is the program now?
- How effective is the program?
- What state, regional, and local documents need to be read as background or will influence the process?
- What is the role of service to the school community?
- How is it influencing teaching and learning?
- What are the local, state, regional, and national documents that impact on the program?

Vision and Mission Statements

- *Mission statement* identifies your long-term support of the mission of the school.
- *Vision statement* identifies who will be affected and why it is important.

Goals and Objectives

- These are the ultimate aims and steps to achieve a dynamic program. Goals are broad statements that envision where the library media program will go over the long term. They flow from the vision and mission statements. The objectives are the steps that need to be taken to reach the goal.

Action Planning

- Provides a step-by-step guide that measures and documents the school library media center's progress toward its goals. These are updated yearly.

Evaluation

- How far have you come?
- What is left to be done?
- How do we continue to move forward?

STEP 1

PLANNING TO PLAN

Who Leads?

In every school several potential leaders may be tapped to assume the responsibility of preparing a school library media program plan. Who is designated depends on the organizational structure of the district, availability of time to effectively lead such a project, and the role that administration decides it should take in the plan's development. Possible choices could include:

- school library media specialist
- library media coordinator
- district library media specialist
- assistant superintendent

Who Is Involved?

It is important that the planning committee represent a wide representation of interested persons, e.g., library staff, teachers, administrators, parents, and users. Consider forming a committee from the following stakeholders:

- superintendent/director
- principal/headmaster
- school committee member/trustee
- library media specialists
- teachers
- IT coordinator
- parents/library volunteers
- students
- public librarian
- curriculum supervisors/department heads

While you may want to offer an open invitation to join the committee, you may find that identifying potential key members is more advantageous. You will want to select committee members who have many or all of the following characteristics:

- Knowledge of the program (or a willingness to learn quickly)
- Time to devote to the project
- A commitment to the planning process
- Political influence
- Communication and/or writing ability
- Willingness to advocate for the plan

Consider how you will involve them. Remember that you will want the committee to "own" the document once it is written, and those individuals who are involved are more apt to take ownership. While you will want a broad cross section of members, remember also that the larger the committee, the more time is consumed in discussion, input, assembling, obtaining consensus, identifying meeting dates, etc. The time frame under which you are working will, in some ways, determine the size of the committee. Prepare a letter, memo, or a phone call of invitation explaining how and why it is important for the invitee to join your team. *Planning templates 1.1 and 1.2 at the end of this chapter will help in this process.*

Prior to a first meeting:

1. Clearly define the role of the committee (Advise? Approve? Prioritize? Identify goals and objectives?).
2. Formulate a draft of an estimated timeline, including a proposed termination date.
3. Think about how many meetings will be involved (group, subcommittee, via e-mail, virtual meetings, etc.).
4. Create an agenda.
5. Provide possible meeting dates, times, and locations.
6. Collect on-hand information about the library program (e.g., library handbook, policies and procedures, collection inventory and/or analysis, copies of communications such as newsletters, and the technology plan).

Brief Description of Plan's Methodology

This section identifies the specifics of the planning process. It informs the reader about how you chose to develop the plan. If you are using the process outlined in this planning document, please refer to it as the **School Library Media Center Long-Range Planning Guide**.

Questions That May Help You Focus Your Thoughts

What is the primary purpose of planning for your library at this time?

_____

_____

_____

Who would be the best committee members? (Names, addresses, phone numbers)

_____

_____

_____

How will you keep everyone informed? (memos, presentations, brief reports, minutes of meetings, etc.)

_____

_____

_____

Can some committee members best contribute by phone or e-mail rather than attend meetings?

_____

_____

_____

List the resources you will need for a successful planning process. Include supplies, materials, advice, assistance, etc.

_____

_____

_____

What is the time frame? The plans and/or updates are due October 1 in order to be able to apply for grants or use it in budget development.

_____

_____

_____

How Complicated Does This Have to Be?

This manual is designed to provide the necessary information, examples, forms, and lists of resources that will provide options for you as you begin the planning process. It is wise to keep it as simple as possible and you may decide that some of the forms in this manual are not necessary in your situation. You will need to decide early in the process whether you need some outside assistance—from others in your library community or a consultant with knowledge of the strategic planning process.

What Does the Plan Have to Include?

The plan must include all of the following elements:

- Brief description of the plan's development and methodology
- Community scan and demographics
- A library mission statement
- Current status—where are we now (needs assessment)
- Multiyear goals and objectives
- Action plan for at least the first year
  - Activities with specific time frames
  - Measures to determine progress
- Approval of the appropriate governing body
- An annual update of the action plan (at the end of each year of operation)

Things to Consider and Answer before You Begin

Have you read *Information Power: Building Partnerships for Learning*? What did you learn from it to help you in thinking about your program? How can it help you educate your school community about the modern role of the library media program?

Have you visited some exemplary school library media programs to explore what your school community might be able to replicate?

What role can the library media program play in the implementation of your curriculum frameworks?

Who should be involved in your school library media center long-range planning?
How do you get them involved?

Do you have community businesses that could be involved? How could you get them involved?

Would the services of a consultant be useful in helping educate the school community to the needs of the library media center program?

PLANNING TEMPLATE 1.1
CONTACTING POTENTIAL COMMITTEE CANDIDATES

Potential Appointee Person to Be Contacted Name/Address/Phone/Email	Person Making Contact (Librarian, Administrator, Coordinator, etc.)	Outcome (Date/Response)

PLANNING TEMPLATE 1.2
INVITATION

Letter of Invitation for Committee Members

The _____ School District wants to develop and maintain quality library media services to meet the needs of our students and the school curriculum under the guidelines of the state frameworks. To that end, school library media centers across the state are embarking on a process to develop three- to five-year plans.

Because we want to achieve broad participation in the development of this long-range plan for _____ School, I am inviting representatives of the school community and staff to join me on the committee. You have been identified as someone who would be able to make a substantial contribution to this effort and be a valuable member of the committee.

The planning committee will assist me in evaluating the current performance of the library media center, studying the library media center's current status, developing goals and objectives in accordance with other planning activities in the system, and prioritizing the library media center roles for the future. The committee will also approve the resulting mission statement, long-range plan, and a year-one action plan based on the long-range plan.

PLANNING TEMPLATE 1.3
INITIAL SUPPORT LETTER

Date:

Dear _____:

The library at _____ is asking for your support to embark on a strategic planning process which will provide an opportunity for the library media center program to:

- Explain your program to others
- Identify priorities, strengths, and weaknesses
- Provide an anchor for developing a budget
- Articulate connections with school's mission
- Provide a blueprint for future development
- Create a clear sense of purpose
- Provide for ongoing evaluation
- Provide a basis for decision making
- Provide a basis for developing accreditation documents or reports
- Provide a foundation for grant writing
- Prove a process for accountability

Your support of this effort on behalf of your library media centers is essential for its success. Good planning takes time—something that is always in short supply. The library media specialist(s) and other key faculty in your **[building, system, or school]** will need to make time to work on the planning committee. Your endorsement of this project would be most welcome. We anticipate the planning process to take between three and six months. We look forward to presenting this to you and other administrators and the school board for approval at that time. To accomplish this we are planning on including many voices on our committee, such as administrators, curriculum leaders, library and technology personnel, parents, students, and community members. Please call if you have any questions.

Respectfully yours,

PLANNING TEMPLATE 1.4
WHO SHOULD . . .

Planning Task	Committee Chair	Committee Member	Library Coordinator	Librarian/LMS	Key Staff	Parent/Volunteer	Other
Read the preliminary documents							
Select the Planning Committee							
Prepare to Keep Stakeholders Informed—Communication Plan							
Develop a Planning Budget							
Set the Planning Timetable							
Orient the Planning Committee							
Articulate a Library Media Center Vision							
Do Community Scan/Adapt from Technology Plan							
Identify School Community Needs							
Conduct Library Scan of Current Status							
Identify Which Community Needs Should Be Addressed							
Write a Library Vision Statement							

(Cont'd)

(Planning Template 1.4, cont'd)

Planning Task	Committee Chair	Committee Member	Library Coordinator	Librarian/LMS	Key Staff	Parent/Volunteer	Other
Write a Library Mission Statement							
Determine Communication Plan to Inform Stakeholders as the Planning Process Progresses							
Set Goals							
Develop a List of Objectives for Each Goal							
Review Measurement and Evaluation Techniques							
Develop a List of Resources Available/Needed							
Craft a List of Activities Needed to Meet Objectives (Action Plan Items)							
Determine Staffing /Resource /Facilities Requirements to Implement Action Plan							
Compile a Draft of the Plan							
Communicate Draft to Stakeholders							
Amend Draft to Create Final Planning Document							
Obtain Final Approval							
Publish and Distribute the Final Plan							

Completed by _____ Library Name _____

Date Completed _____

PLANNING TEMPLATE 1.5
PLANNING CALENDAR AND TASK ASSIGNMENTS

TASK	Assigned to (Person)	1	2	3	4	5	6	7	8	9	10	11	12
Read the preliminary documents													
Select the Planning Committee													
Develop a Planning Budget													
Set the Planning Timetable													
Prepare for Keeping Stakeholders Informed— Communication Plan													
Orient the Planning Committee													
Articulate a Library Media Center Vision													
Do Community Scan/Adapt Technology Plan's Scan													
Identify School Community Needs													
Conduct Library Scan of Current Status													
Identify Which Community Needs Should Be Addressed													
Write a Library Vision Statement													
Write a Library Mission Statement													
Determine Communication Plan to Inform Stakeholders as the Planning Process Progresses													

(Cont'd)

(Planning Template 1.5, cont'd)

TASK	Assigned to (Person)	1	2	3	4	5	6	7	8	9	10	11	12
Set Goals													
Develop a List of Objectives for Each Goal													
Review Measurement and Evaluation Techniques													
Develop a List of Resources Available/Needed													
Craft a List of Activities Needed to Meet Objectives (Action Plan Items)													
Determine Staffing/ Resource/Facilities Requirements Needed to Implement Action Plan													
Compile a Draft of the Plan													
Communicate Draft to Stakeholders													
Amend Draft to Create Final Planning Document													
Obtain Final Approval													

Completed by _____   Library Name _____

Date Completed _____

PLANNING TEMPLATE 1.6
PLANNING BUDGET

Budget Category	Number	Estimated Unit Cost	Cost
Example			
Refreshments for committee meetings	8	$20.00	$160.00

Committee Support

    Planning materials _____ _____ _____

    Resources _____ _____ _____

    Photocopies (minutes,
    orientation documents,
    planning templates, draft plan) _____ _____ _____

    Postage _____ _____ _____

    Refreshments _____ _____ _____

    Supplies _____ _____ _____

    Information/PR _____ _____ _____

    Other _____ _____ _____

Consultants/Facilitators

    Fees _____ _____ _____

    Travel expenses _____ _____ _____

Staff Expenses

    Substitutes _____ _____ _____

    Secretarial assistance _____ _____ _____

Printing the Plan

    Final plan _____ _____ _____

    Promotional materials _____ _____ _____

TOTAL _____

PLANNING TEMPLATE 1.7
COMMUNICATION PLAN

Concept/Information to Be Shared	When	By Whom	To Whom	Where/How

STEP 2

Connecting with the School's Mission and Community

It is essential that any plan actively support the mission of the school and meet the aspirations of the community. This mission guides the development of the curriculum, defines how the school envisions the accomplishment of its vision, and establishes how the various activities and departments of the school contribute to this vision.

Key to this, in today's world, is the understanding of your state or district curriculum frameworks. These curriculum guides rest on a common core of learning, and define "curriculum" in your state or region. Alongside this state or district guideline stand the state and national standards for the profession and the accreditation documents, which provide an additional frame of reference for action within the profession.

Documents that can assist in the understanding of the school's mission are the accreditation philosophy statements. These are generally developed for high school accreditation self-studies and articulate the aspirations of the secondary (or other levels) school community for its learners. While middle and elementary schools may have similar documents, a district plan could find the high school's work instructive to the process.

> **Documents Needed**
>
> - **State or District Curriculum Frameworks**
> - **School's Philosophy Statement**
> - **District Technology Plan**
> - *Information Power*
> - **School Library Media Center Standards**
> - **Accreditation Self-Study Report**

In addition, in schools that have developed technology plans, these documents can provide solid assistance in the planning for school library media centers. Many, if not most, mention the library media center program as a part of their overall information technology plan for the schools. Although few, if any, have included any meaningful detail, it is important for the school library media center [strategic] plan to be coordinated with the school's technology plan.

Current technology plans provide necessary demographic data and a descriptive overview of the district as a whole. Individual school variations from this norm should be described in a single sheet detailing the individual differences that may influence a library media center program in a particular school building.

A community scan provides up-to-date information about the composition of your school community. It describes the community, the learners, the faculty, and the teaching strategies, and takes into account other information and technology programs in the school. You should

> **It is important that you know where you are in order to plan for the future.**

include any special needs that your school serves, as well as any elements that make your school unique. Be sure to consult the Technology Plan in your district, since much of the work may have been done for you in that document.

School's Mission and Philosophy Statements

Summarize the school's mission and philosophy, using the documents prepared for the accreditation process. It is important that the school library media program's mission and philosophy be closely aligned with those of the school as a whole.

Description of Your School Community

Provide a brief description of the demographics of your city, town, or school community. This gives a picture of the setting in which the school functions. Information for this can be extracted from various departments of education in individual states.

_____

_____

_____

_____

Impact of State Testing

If your state has a state testing or state school evaluation process, these documents can provide some guidance or an impetus for change in a number of areas of school operation including the library media program. For example, if reading scores were unsatisfactory, perhaps that should become an area for particular attention, or the scores may indicate that the skills sequence requires adjustment to assure that the information skills expected match the time frames in which they are being introduced and practiced.

_____

_____

_____

_____

PLANNING TEMPLATE 2.1
COMMUNITY SCAN FOR INDIVIDUAL SCHOOLS
(District Plan Supplement)

Answering the following questions will help you develop your individual school library media center description.

How many children attend your school? _____

What grade levels does your school serve? _____

Please describe your community. Include demographics, such as population, location, total area, race and ethnicity, income distribution, educational level of the community, money per pupil for schools, the extent of parental involvement, etc.

_____

_____

_____

_____

Are there any special programs in the school?

_____

_____

_____

_____

Are there any special-needs programs?

_____

_____

_____

_____

What makes your school unique? For example, does it have a special mission, special populations, particular problems, etc.?

_____

_____

_____

_____

Provide a brief summary of the results of state testing and the impact of testing on the community and on the school—and what the implications might be, therefore, for the school library media program.

_____

_____

_____

_____

STEP 3

VISION STATEMENT

A vision statement is a set of words or precepts you can put together so that you are focusing on a distantly achievable goal. Vision statements address four major questions:

1. Who will benefit?

2. What will the benefit be?

3. What is the result of the benefit?

4. Why is the result of the benefit important?

A vision for the school library media center is noted in *Information Literacy Standards for Student Learning*, (ALA, 1998) as "the ability to find and use information . . . the keystone of lifelong learning" (ASCD quote). All of the activities inherent in today's library media program are focused on providing students with the skills, knowledge, resources, and environment in which this vision can flourish. The program has moved from one of curriculum support to that of interdependence with the instructional program, to provide future citizens with the intellectual and technical skills to succeed in an information society.

> *Who benefits?*
> Students
>
> *What will the benefit be?*
> Efficient, effective, and astute users of information
>
> *What is the result?*
> Students will be informed, active lifelong learners.
>
> *Why is the result important?*
> Preparing contributing members of society; career success in an ever-changing global village; able to satisfy their own curiosity.

The results of the focus groups clearly identified two additional vision statements, one emphasizing an institutional vision and the other a rewording of the national standards that focuses on student learning. These visions were:

School library media center programs empower the curricula and frameworks.

and

School library media center programs promote and teach information literacy skills that encompass the ability to find, use, and evaluate ideas and information, leading to productive lifelong learning.

While a vision statement may be considered optional in some planning documents, it truly forms the cornerstone for the library media program and is an important and integral step in the planning process.

Things to Consider and Answer before You Begin

- What is your vision of what the library media program could be in your school?

- As a result of the completion of this long-range plan, how will your situation be different three to five years from now?

- What will teachers/staff members be saying or doing differently?

- What will students be saying or doing differently?

Sample Vision Statements

1. The Sycamore Elementary School Library Media Program promotes and teaches information literacy skills so that students will become efficient, effective, and astute users of information. With these skills they will become informed, active, lifelong learners. They will be contributing members of society who can achieve career success in an ever-changing world, and satisfy their own curiosity about that world, acquiring an understanding of and appreciation for the varieties of the human condition.

2. The Dearborn Middle School Library Media Center program works to develop lifelong learners. It supports the school's curricula and the frameworks; promotes teaching the information literacy skills of locating, evaluating, and using ideas and information; and fosters lifelong learning. National and state information literacy standards for student learning guide the library media program. Students are encouraged to perceive reading and information seeking as lifelong activities. The media center, through its program, becomes the learning laboratory of the school—everyone's classroom—that fosters collaboration among teachers and students.

3. The Upland High School Library Media and Technology Program is an integral part of the teaching and learning process and is essential to developing lifelong learners, independent thinkers and problem solvers in a complex information society. By playing a central role in the teaching and learning process, the program empowers the school's curriculum to respond to and cultivate an authentic, information- and resource-based learning environment.

STEP 4

ESSENTIAL ELEMENTS AND CURRENT STATUS

Needs Assessment

In this step, you will be assessing your school library media center's current situation and services first from your personal point of view; later you will have committee members do a similar assessment. It is important to recognize that divergent opinions may arise as committee members see things through a different set of lenses. The outcome of this analysis of current conditions is often called a "needs assessment." In order to establish a more consistent assessment, a basic set of rubrics, which may be used or expanded, is provided in this section.

Essential Elements

National and state guidelines provide a framework for essential elements of school library media programs. In *Information Power* (ALA, 1998) these are grouped into three major areas:

- Teaching and learning
  - Collaborative planning and teaching
  - Individual and collaborative student inquiry
  - Information literacy skills
  - Staff development
    - Faculty
    - Librarian

- Information access and delivery
  - Curriculum-based collection development
  - Technological access (including resource automation)
  - Collaboration with other institutions and agencies
  - Intellectual Freedom and atmosphere for learning

- Program administration
  - Professional staffing plus appropriate support staff
  - Facility appropriate to learning
  - Financial support
  - Communication and advocacy
    - Policies, procedures, and practice

These components are considered essential to the delivery of minimum levels of service to the school community and were validated by the findings of the regional focus groups. Rank your current school library media center in terms of these essential elements using the rubric provided at the end of this section. Give your library a **4** for **outstanding**, a **3** for **satisfactory**, a **2** for **needs improvement**, and a **1** for each **unsatisfactory** element. While these elements should be present in any school or district, various grade levels may place different emphasis on each element.

Essential Elements	4	3	2	1
Collaborative Planning and Teaching				
Individual and Collaborative Student Inquiry				
Integrated Information Literacy Skills				
Professional Growth and Development				
Curriculum Based Collection Development				
Technological Access (automation, resources)				
Collaboration with Other Institutions and Agencies				
Intellectual Freedom				
Professional Staffing and Appropriate Support Staff				
Facility Appropriate to Learning				
Financial Support				
Communication and Advocacy				

Current Status

The current status is determined by asking the question: Where are you now? Thus begins your analysis of the state of current practices, services, policies, procedures, staffing, and resources that will enable the program to achieve its vision. Once this baseline is established, a foundation has been built that can lead to the development of budgets, growth, and change. The library media center then can turn to various guidelines and standards to see how the current and proposed improvements overlay the expected or recommended norms.

> **Where are you now?**

Knowing what you have in place includes not only resources within the school department, but also resources from outside agencies, such as the public library, that are, or can be, devoted to the implementation of the proposed program. This then determines what additional services or resources are needed and the impact of these (funding, personnel, equipment, space, etc.) to make the vision a reality. You should include initial, one-time-only, and on-going costs for operating the program or implementing the change. Do not forget to include consideration of the needs relative to technology as well as the guidelines/requirements of the Americans with Disabilities Act (ADA). When ready to make suggestions, be sure to create a prioritized list of the envisioned improvements and enhancements to the program that you have identified.

Things to Consider and Answer before You Begin

- What services might you be able to initiate to help increase basic literacy?

- Are information literacy skills embedded within the curricula of most disciplines in your school?

- What is the condition of your collection? What needs to be done to improve it?

- Is the faculty involved with the library media specialist in collection development?

- Is there a collection development plan in place?

- Is the collection of sufficient breadth and currency to be pertinent to the school's program of studies?

- Is the library media center involved with the storage and circulation of computer software?

- Is the library media center involved in the record keeping required for computer software site licensing?

- Has the school library media center been able to develop multicultural resources? If not, should that be a priority now?

- Has your school library media center been automated? How could automation enhance your school library media program?

- Where is the library media center's involvement with technology? What electronic resources are available for students and staff? Is the Internet available? How is access obtained? Are teachers and students learning how to efficiently and effectively access information from electronic resources? What electronic library resources are available throughout the whole school? What are your equipment, electronic database, and software needs?

- Is technology seen as a vital tool for information problem solving?

- What are your space needs?

- What are your renovation needs?

- What are your furniture needs?

- What are the staff development/training needs of the school library media specialist, library staff, teachers, and the principal?

- How is school release time currently used? Could it be used to help facilitate staff development in the access and use of information via the resources available in the library media center?

- What is the level of parental involvement? Could parents be tapped to help with some of the needs of the school library media center?

- What are the staffing levels and personnel needs to be able to carry out the tasks inherent in the type of program envisioned?

- Has the library media specialist been involved in curriculum planning? If not, how could the library media specialist become involved?

- Do you have an effective library media advocacy program? What would you need to do to put one in place?

Description of the Library Media Program

Briefly describe your library media program as it currently exists.

_____

_____

_____

_____

What special programs does your library media center provide?

_____

_____

_____

_____

How do students get access to the library media center?

_____

_____

How do teachers access the services of the library media center and of the library media specialist?

_____

_____

_____

Are you working on developing a flexibly accessed library media program? If yes, how?

_____

_____

_____

Is the library media specialist involved in cooperative planning with the classroom teachers?

_____

_____

_____

_____

Is the library media specialist involved in curriculum development with the classroom teachers?

_____

_____

_____

_____

Describe how technology is integrated into the library media program.

_____

_____

_____

_____

Describe library media center involvement with the reading program and literacy development in the school.

_____

_____

What is the budget for the school library media center? (Include breakdown by categories.)

_____

_____

Assessment Rubrics

The term "rubric" originated from the Latin, *rubrica*, meaning "red clay." In early times, this red clay was used to mark important things; eventually red clay led to red wax seals, which protected the contents of written correspondence.

Rubrics provide librarians with **specific criteria** for evaluating components of the program, products (PR documents, bookmarks, bibliographies, etc.), or performance. In addition they provide a tool that increases the consistency of the evaluation among evaluators (teachers, librarians, administrators, students, parents, etc.) as well as **provide clear targets** for program improvement.

TRAITS / SCALE	Understanding	Frequency	Effectiveness	Independence
4	Thorough/ Complete	Usually/ Consistently	Highly Effective	Independently
3	Substantial	Frequently	Effective	With Minimal Assistance
2	Partial / Incomplete	Sometimes	Barely Effective	With Moderate Assistance
1	Misundestood/ Serious Misconceptions	Rarely/Never	Ineffective	Only with Considerable Assistance

Wiggins and McTighe (1998)

Rubric Examples

If one were to examine each **essential element** to determine how the school library media center assesses its performance, you would decide which *trait(s)* best fits the element, develop a sentence using the terminology of the trait, and then develop a statement that defines each scale level. Some essential elements could lend themselves to more than one trait. The following rubrics provide a starting point by providing one rubric for each of the essential element's primary trait. Please feel free to modify these for local application.

Planning templates of blank rubrics will assist in developing additional rubrics, should you choose to do so.

For example, using the *effectiveness* trait for the essential element:

Collaborative Planning and Teaching

TRAIT/SCALE *Effectiveness*	PERFORMANCE DESCRIPTOR	BENCHMARK
Highly Effective 4	The LMS and teacher *exhibit highly effective* collaboration and planning on units and lessons.	The LMS and teacher co-plan units and lessons, meeting regularly in advance to identify strategies and resources.
Effective 3	The LMS and teacher exhibit *effective* collaboration and planning on units and lessons.	The LMS and teacher meet prior to the development of units, lesson plans, and class visits.
Barely Effective 2	The LMS and teacher do superficial collaboration and planning on units and lessons.	The LMS and teacher do some advance planning; the teacher sends assignments in advance of class visits.
Ineffective 1	The LMS and teacher exhibit *ineffective* collaboration and planning on units and lessons.	The LMS is not involved in the planning; classes arrive unannounced, or with little or no preparation possible on the part of the LMS.

Individual Student Inquiry

TRAIT/SCALE *Independence*	PERFORMANCE DESCRIPTOR	BENCHMARK
Independently 4	The student is able to determine the question to be answered, its essential components and leads to meaningful information selection, evaluation, and use.	The student can construct a search strategy and find, evaluate, and use the appropriate data.
With Minimal Assistance 3	The student begins by identifying a question and makes decisions by gathering and considering relevant information.	The student is able to construct a search strategy but has difficulty selecting, evaluating, and organizing the data.
With Moderate Assistance 2	The student considers the topic focus and "under direction" will find readily available resources.	The student is able to identify a search strategy, locate, select, and analyze appropriate information with assistance.
Only With Considerable Assistance 1	The student researches a generic topic and uses the easiest and most readily available source.	The student is unable to develop a search strategy or to identify or select appropriate information.

Integrated Information Literacy Skills

TRAIT/SCALE *Effectiveness*	PERFORMANCE DESCRIPTOR	BENCHMARK
Highly Effective **4**	All skills are introduced and practiced through classroom assignments.	Instructional units are planned and always incorporate information literacy skills.
Effective **3**	A continuum of information skills is often integrated into classroom activities and assignments.	A progression of skills is incorporated over time into a library instructional framework and systematically with all students.
Barely Effective **2**	Assignments occasionally include information skills.	Skills are taught in random fashion to ever changing groups of students, often without reference to class assignments or current activities.
Ineffective **1**	Information skills are taught in isolation of classroom activities and assignments.	The library skills program is fixed in content and sequence and provides preparation time for teachers.

Professional Growth and Development

TRAIT/SCALE *Understanding*	PERFORMANCE DESCRIPTOR	BENCHMARK
Thorough and Complete 4	The library media specialist actively participates in performance evaluation and professional activities.	The library media specialist enjoys leadership positions in professional organizations, regularly reads professional journals and takes advantage of professional growth opportunities.
Substantial 3	The library media specialist joins professional organizations and attends required in-service.	The library media specialist takes advantage of professional opportunities on a regular basis.
Partial/ Incomplete 2	The library media specialist attends required in-service.	The library media specialist takes minimal advantage of professional opportunities.
Misunderstood/ Serious Misconceptions 1	The library media specialist assumes that continuing education is irrelevant or a waste of time.	The library media specialist avoids participation in in-service and course work related to the profession as educator or library media specialist.

Curriculum-Based Collection Development

TRAIT/SCALE *Effectiveness*	PERFORMANCE DESCRIPTOR	BENCHMARK
Highly Effective **4**	The library media specialist is knowledgeable about the curriculum, the frameworks, the publishers and producers of high-quality resources and works within the construct of a selection policy.	The high-quality collection includes many formats, uses data from the automation system, and maintains strong curriculum emphasis gleaned from extensive communication with the faculty.
Effective **3**	The library media specialist systematically updates areas of the collection using characteristics of the highly effective traits (above).	Many but not all of the traits shown above are used to develop the collection.
Barely Effective **2**	The library media specialist has limited knowledge of the curriculum and frameworks, a process for collection development, and an outdated selection policy.	The collection is uneven in its currency and quality, lacks appropriate formats as well as direct connections to the curriculum.
Ineffective **1**	The library media specialist has no systematic process for keeping the collection current, uses catalogs in lieu of selection tools, and has no selection policy.	There is no reliable currency or quality.

Technology Access

TRAIT/SCALE Effectiveness	PERFORMANCE DESCRIPTOR	BENCHMARK
Highly Effective **4**	The library media center has reliable access to automated resources, the WWW, and other electronic resources both inside and outside of the school.	Students and faculty have dependable access to information throughout the day and from home.
Effective **3**	The library media center has automated its collection, has limited access to the WWW, and in-school access only to electronic resources.	Students and faculty have limited or unreliable access from class and/or the LMC throughout the day.
Barely Effective **2**	The library media center has automated, purchases few electronic resources, and limits access to the WWW.	Students and faculty must come to the library to use the limited resources available and to access the WWW.
Ineffective **1**	The library media center has not automated and access to the Web or electronic information is problematic.	Students and faculty must use the card catalog to access the collection; few electronic resources are provided and Web access is limited.

Collaboration with Other Institutions and Agencies

TRAIT/SCALE Understanding	PERFORMANCE DESCRIPTOR	BENCHMARK
Thorough and Complete **4**	The library media specialist recognizes the universality of information and creates an outreach program to connect with other libraries, museums, agencies and information specialists in the community or region.	The library media center actively encourages students and faculty to access other appropriate information institutions and agencies.
Substantial **3**	The library media specialist coordinates an outreach program with the local public library and other local agencies.	There is systematic and regular communication and information sharing between the public library, local agencies, and the school including interlibrary loan services.
Partial/ Incomplete **2**	The library media specialist communicates occasionally with the public library.	Limited information is shared between the school and the local public library.
Misunderstood/ Serious Miscon- ceptions **1**	The library media specialist adopts a "go-it-alone" attitude toward other agencies.	Students and faculty find no assistance if what they need is not available in their local school library.

Intellectual Freedom

TRAIT/SCALE *Understanding*	PERFORMANCE DESCRIPTOR	BENCHMARK
Thorough and Complete 4	The library media specialist understands and endorses the ALA Bill of Rights and provides as open access as possible under the law.	Students and faculty have unfettered access to information.* *Under current federal law filters are generally required.
Substantial 3	The library media specialist understands and endorses the ALA Bill of Rights with reservations related to age appropriateness of materials. Condones customizing the filtering of the WWW.	Students and faculty have generally open access to information after due consideration of age appropriateness.
Partial / Incomplete 2	The library media specialist has reservations about open access and restricts some topics. Accepts the limitation of the filter.	Students and faculty have to request certain topics from a closed collection.
Misunderstood/ Serious Misconceptions 1	The library media specialist censors materials in the selection process in order to ensure no controversies.	The student and faculty have access only to those materials the library media specialist considers safe.

Professional Staffing and Appropriate Support Staff

TRAIT/SCALE *Effectiveness*	PERFORMANCE DESCRIPTOR	BENCHMARK
Highly Effective **4**	Certified professional, non-professional, and technical staff meet national standards and are available before, after, and throughout the school day.	Students and faculty can meet at their convenience to co-plan instruction and rely on immediate assistance.
Effective **3**	The certified professional, non-professional, and technical staff are sufficient to provide reliable and consistent access for students and faculty throughout the school day.	Students and faculty can schedule time, develop units, and receive assistance without undue delay.
Barely Effective **2**	The certified professional, non-professional and technical staff are able to juggle the activities and needs of students and faculty.	Students and faculty have difficulty scheduling, meeting with, or receiving assistance or instruction from appropriate staff.
Ineffective **1**	The certified professional, non-professional and technical staff are insufficient to accommodate the needs of students and faculty.	Students and faculty find the staff unavailable or available only for limited time and activities.

Facility Appropriate to Learning

TRAIT/SCALE *Effectiveness*	PERFORMANCE DESCRIPTOR	BENCHMARK
Highly Effective **4**	**The facility is welcoming, well-managed, accommodates simultaneous activities, and has reliable technology, and a well-designed instructional area.**	**Students and faculty find all aspects of the facility enhance their teaching and learning.**
Effective 3	**The facility is welcoming, well-managed, has reliable technology and accommodates a limited number of students.**	**Students and faculty must book far in advance to use the facility.**
Barely Effective 2	**The facility can accommodate only some of the learning and teaching activities requested.**	**The students and faculty use the LMC only when other options are not available.**
Ineffective 1	**Little use is made of the instructional potential because students/faculty feel uncomfortable, technology is unreliable, and layout does not support simultaneous use.**	**Students make little use of the facility and its resources; faculty do not incorporate information literacy skills into their assignments and activities.**

Financial Support

TRAIT/SCALE *Effectiveness*	PERFORMANCE DESCRIPTOR	BENCHMARK
Highly Effective 4	The library media specialist prepares a realistic budget based on planning and recommends adequate funding for all aspects of the program.	The administration supports and recognizes the need to maintain a highly responsive library media center to meet student and faculty teaching and learning demands.
Effective 3	The library media specialist proposes a budget and negotiates with the administration for the priorities.	Administration encourages input into the budget process and advocates for the program.
Barely Effective 2	The library media specialist provides minimal input to the budget process.	Budgets are presented to administration with insufficient rationale, few initiatives, and are expected to be cut or are simple reiterations of the previous year's budget.
Ineffective 1	The library media specialist has little or no input into the development of the library media center's budget for the school.	Systematic updating, planned program initiatives reflecting shifts in teaching strategies, and curriculum requirements are not supported.

Communication and Advocacy

TRAIT/SCALE *Frequency*	PERFORMANCE DESCRIPTOR	BENCHMARK
Usually and Consistently 4	The library media specialist develops and implements a comprehensive communication plan for the school community and evaluates its effectiveness.	Faculty, students, and administrators are aware of all aspects of the school library media program and its role in the teaching and learning process.
Frequently 3	The library media specialist develops and implements a communication plan for the school community and evaluates its effectiveness.	Faculty, students, and administrators kept informed of some aspects of the school library media program and its role in the teaching and learning process.
Occasionally 2	The library media specialist develops and implements a communication plan for the school community.	Faculty, students, and administrators are sporadically informed of particular program activities.
Rarely or Never 1	The library media specialist occasionally sends out newsletters to the school community.	The school community is generally uninformed about current or anticipated library program initiatives.

PLANNING TEMPLATE 4.1
EFFECTIVENESS RUBRIC

TRAIT/SCALE *Effectiveness*	PERFORMANCE DESCRIPTOR	BENCHMARK
Highly Effective 4		
Effective 3		
Barely Effective 2		
Ineffective 1		

PLANNING TEMPLATE 4.2
UNDERSTANDING RUBRIC

TRAIT/SCALE Understanding	PERFORMANCE DESCRIPTOR	BENCHMARK
Thorough and Complete 4		
Substantial 3		
Partial / Incomplete 2		
Misunderstood/ Serious Misconceptions 1		

PLANNING TEMPLATE 4.3
FREQUENCY RUBRIC

TRAIT/SCALE Frequency	PERFORMANCE DESCRIPTOR	BENCHMARK
Usually and Consistently 4		
Frequently 3		
Occasionally 2		
Rarely or Never 1		

PLANNING TEMPLATE 4.4
INDEPENDENCE RUBRIC

TRAIT/SCALE *Independence*	PERFORMANCE DESCRIPTOR	BENCHMARK
Independently **4**		
With Minimal Assistance **3**		
With Moderate Assistance **2**		
Only With Considerable Assistance **1**		

STEP 5

MISSION STATEMENT

The Mission Statement

The mission statement represents the school library media center's reason for being. A good mission statement should accurately explain why your school library media center exists and what it hopes to achieve in the future. It articulates the organization's essential nature, its values, and its work. It should be free of jargon. The mission statement is the heart of the *Strategic* plan of the school library media center. The mission statement should answer the following questions:

- What are the opportunities or needs that we exist to address? (The purpose of the organization.)
- What are we doing to address these needs? (The business of the organization.)
- What principles or beliefs guide our work? (The values of the organization.)

Information Power (1998) expresses the school library media program's mission as "ensuring that students and staff are effective users of ideas and information." It further notes that "this mission is accomplished

- by providing intellectual and physical access to materials in all formats,
- by providing instruction to foster competence and stimulate interest in reading, viewing, and using information and ideas, [and]
- by working with other educators to design learning strategies to meet the needs of individual students."

The focus group developed the following list of reasons why the school library media center exists, and what purposes it serves within the school community. Your school may have more to add to this list. Some items may relate more to particular grade levels or situations. The overwhelming support was for priority mission statements 1 through 4, as they encompass much of the "instructional role" of the library media center program.

Priority	Purpose of LMC (Mission)
1	Provide Foundation of Skills and Knowledge for Enjoying and Using Ideas and Information
2	Empower the School's Curriculum
3	Teach Information Literacy Strategies and Techniques to Promote Efficient and Effective Use of Information
4	Support the Mission of the School
5	Foster a Love of Reading
6	Develop Lifelong Learners
7	Foster Intellectual Curiosity
8	Facilitate the Ever-Changing Information Environment
9	Develop Diverse Collections in Many Formats to Meet Learning Styles of Students
10	Support Good Instruction
11	Provide a Sanctuary for Students Needing Attention, Help, Quiet, Involvement, Intellectual Stimulation, or "Something Different"
12	Provide Literature and Reading Guidance

Priority Missions of School Library Media Center Services

The mission statements of the school library media center (SLMC) provide a focus for establishing the goals of the SLMC program of services.

The first four missions are closely related to the information society in which students live, work, and, in the future, will prosper. They also anchor the changed role of the library media center program and the role of the library media specialist in a twenty-first-century school. These "information literacy" skills form the backbone of knowledge about how to function in the twenty-first-century workplace. Competencies that support this role that have been taken from the NEEMA *Final Report* (1998) can be found in appendix A, under the headings of "Criteria and Indicators."

As with all aspects of the educational process the school library media center plays a role in the empowering of the school's curriculum. The program should be carefully crafted to follow the philosophy and dictums of the school curriculum, particularly as we move toward inquiry-based and resource-based learning environments. Carefully selected collections of resources, both in the school and accessed from external sources, support the classroom instructional activities in ways heretofore impossible. The advent of technology has made this changed teaching and learning environment possible.

The library media center program provides a degree of equity around access to technology, and as such, seeks to direct and organize both the effective and efficient use of the information. The "mechanical" access to external sources is reasonably simplistic and dependent on the hardware and infrastructure investment; the "intellectual" access to these same sources depends on new strategies and techniques that must be taught—they are not intuitive. This is one way that the library media center program and the school's mission of teaching and learning become interdependent.

Again, the mechanics of teaching the decoding process in learning to read is well-handled by the classroom. The joy of reading happens when children take advantage of personal choices, exploring a wide range of experiences that exposes them to fine literature and at the same time provide them with a cultural literary heritage. Whether the literatures are fact, fiction, print, visual or aural is essentially immaterial—as long as the joys of reading, viewing, listening and learning are actively pursued throughout one's lifetime. Creating an atmosphere in which this is encouraged has become part of the library media center's role.

With the plethora of information available, one has opportunities to explore ideas in great depth and breadth. Fostering a broad exploration into the expanding universe of information stimulates the development of a lifelong intellectual curiosity.

There is no inherent stability in today's information environment. Change will accelerate, rather than diminish. The shift from a linear information model, such as a book, to a multimedia and, more recently, to hypertext requires new thinking and techniques, and ultimately, new ways of learning. The hypertext environment is associative rather than linear in its organization. Teaching the skills and concepts that will assist students in working productively within this new environment has become the responsibility and role of the school library media specialist.

Multilingual and multicultural collections in a wide variety of formats allow students to access ideas and concepts in ways that more closely meet their own personal learning styles. We are continually learning more about how our minds work and how students and teachers learn. Resources are being acquired to better meet the demands of a wide variety of learning styles.

Resource collections in school library media centers provide a foundation for the newer teaching techniques, such as inquiry and resource-based learning. Good instruction relies on the support from and integration of this wide information base.

The social function of the school library media center is interwoven with its instructional function. It provides a sanctuary for students needing specialized or unique attention, general assistance, or simply a place to work (sometimes a quiet place!).

The specialized knowledge of resources that the school library media specialists bring to their role within the school community provides a basis for identifying key resources to meet the goals and objectives of the faculty and students. Not only must they keep up with publishing trends and the various literatures for children, but also be able provide literature and reading guidance services to keep fellow professionals aware of what is available on a variety of topics, in what formats, as well as what choices teachers and students have in identifying quality resources that meet their needs.

Missions

Consider how your library media center carries out the mission statements (Purpose of the Library Media Center) above. *Refer to planning templates 5.1 and 5.2.*

PLANNING TEMPLATE 5.1
MISSION STATEMENTS

Create a worksheet based on these missions as they apply to your library. Ask staff, teachers, volunteers, students, etc., to list any words, phrases, or ideas that come to mind with respect to the school library media center and these various items. Give everyone a chance to be heard. Look for language and concepts that enjoy great repetition.

Questions you may want to use:

- What visible indicators are there concerning the importance of this purpose?
- Does the school library media center have a special collection emphasis that supports this purpose?
- How does the available space and layout impact this purpose?
- Does the library give this purpose a major emphasis? No emphasis?

LMC Purpose [Opportunities and Needs]	How Does this Fit the School Mission?	What Activities Address this Purpose?

PLANNING TEMPLATE 5.2
MISSION STATEMENT EVALUATION

Existing mission statement: _____

_____

_____

_____

Significant changes since the last planning cycle:

_____

_____

_____

Aspects of the existing mission that are still appropriate:

_____

_____

_____

Aspects of the existing mission statement that are no longer appropriate or need to be changed:

_____

_____

_____

Recommended changes in wording the existing mission statement:

_____

_____

Sample Mission Statements

1. The library media program must enable students and staff members to effectively locate, evaluate, use, and create information. The library media specialist does this by providing access to information resources in a variety of media formats, providing instruction and assistance to promote information literacy, encouraging an interest in reading and using information and ideas. Collaborating with other educators to develop curriculum that meets educational standards and the individual needs of the students is essential to creating instruction that presents information literacy skills in meaningful situations for the students. In this way the library media program will assist the students and staff in becoming effective users and creators of information.

2. Sinclair SLMC is the information laboratory of the school, fostering intellectual curiosity, enjoyment of reading, and lifelong learning in an inviting, stimulating, and enriching environment. Students and teachers engage in information retrieval. The SLMC instructional program teaches information literacy strategies and techniques to empower discriminating consumers and to promote the efficient and effective use of this information in an inquiry and resource-based learning and teaching environment. The SLMC provides intellectual and physical access to information and ideas.

3. The Library Media and Technology Program of the Connor School Library Media Center creates a foundation for lifelong learning, critical thinking, and problem solving. To ensure that students and teachers are effective and efficient users and producers of information, the program provides all members of the school community equal access to a wide range of services, activities, resources, and educational technologies. This mission is accomplished through goals in the following three areas: learning and teaching; information access and delivery; and program administration.

4. The mission of the school library media center (SLMC) program is to ensure that students and staff are effective users of ideas and information. This mission shall be accomplished by providing intellectual and physical access to materials in all formats; by providing instruction to foster competence and stimulate interest in reading, viewing, and using information and ideas; and by working with other educators to design learning strategies to meet the needs of individual students.

STEP 6

GOALS AND OBJECTIVES

Establishing multiyear goals and objectives as well as the measurements you will need to assess progress is important. It is also important to differentiate progress from movement. Often, in the busy day-to-day life of the school library media center, movement overwhelms progress. The difference is between marching in place and marching forward. They feel the same, but only one makes any real difference!

Multiyear Projections—Goals and Objectives

In order to project where you want to be in the years ahead, it is essential that you set goals. These are the broad statements that describe the envisioned ends toward which the library media center will work over the long-term. These can be expressed from the point of view of the school library media center (management or organization), from a service point of view (services and resources), or from the student, faculty, or administrators' point of view. Goals should flow logically from the vision and mission statements. A goal is normally not measurable, may take years of planning to achieve, or may never be fully reached. However, goals will probably not change over a three- to five-year period. Goals define your chosen course of action for meeting the needs of your school community. The school library media center may want to establish two sets of goals:

> - **Where do you want to go?**
> - **What do you want to see students doing in the school library media center in the years ahead?**

- Program-oriented goals—describe components of the program of services for the faculty and students.

- Management or organizational goals—describe managerial and organizational components of the library media center program.

However, it is essential to recognize that management and organizational goals are undertaken to improve the conditions for delivering the program. They are inexorably linked to the ultimate end—that of providing improved programs of service to our school community.

> - **What steps must be taken to reach the goal?**
> - **What activities are in place or need to be developed?**
> - **How will they be measured?**

Objectives are specific short-range statements of results to be achieved to implement a goal. Objectives begin with an action verb, deal with only one idea each, are measurable, include time frames and are attainable. An objective focuses on the "end result," and specifies **what** and **when**, but not **why** or **how**. Specific activities expand the detail, define the **how** and **why** it is important, **who** is charged with the responsibility for seeing it through, and under what conditions. Objectives may or may not change over a three- to five-year period depending upon progress made. There are times in the life of a school when events over which one has little or no control intrude. In such cases, objectives may not meet an established time frame. In such instances, a revised objective or an extension of the time frame may be entirely appropriate. The achievement of the objectives inherently moves one closer to the stated goal. Together, the goals and objectives comprise the *operational* plan for the library media center.

OBJECTIVE: What and When

ACTION PLAN: How, Why, and Who

Sample Goals and Objectives

Program Goal

To provide a collection of resources in a variety of formats that reflects the science and technology frameworks and meets the needs of the middle school students.

Objectives

1.1   By **[provide date—next school year]**, the science and technology collections will meet current state library media standards.

1.2   By **[provide date—next school year]**, all topics and concepts in the curriculum frameworks will have sufficient resources to meet 90 percent of the information requests of students.

Activities	Description	Timeline	Who Is Responsible	Resources Req'd. Resources est. Cost	Measure
1.1	Review the Science and Technology Frameworks	End of September	Library Media Specialist	Frameworks documents from state	Report of findings
1.2	Review existing holdings against Frameworks topics and concepts	September– October	Library Media Specialist	None	Report of findings
1.3	Solicit teacher input on selections	October– November	Library Media Specialist	None	Suggested list for ordering
1.4	Expand resources on topics and concepts identified as lacking depth	October– December	Library Media Specialist	Bibliographies of recommended titles Est. $200	Develop and order list of recommended titles Est. $600–$2000

Organizational Goal

To provide professional assistance to students throughout the day by providing an adequate number of motivated, enthusiastic staff members with appropriate skills and training.

Objectives

1.1   By **[provide date—next school year]**, the library will have adequate staff with appropriate skills and training to meet the needs of an inquiry-based curriculum.

1.2   Each staff member will have a minimum of four hours of in-house technology training that she or he will evaluate as useful.

1.3   By **[provide date—next school year]**, the school library will have developed a staffing plan to meet standards.

Activities	Description	Timeline	Who Is Responsible	Resources Required $ est.	Output
1.1	Analyze staffing pattern, responsibilities, and schedule	January	Library Media Specialist	None	Report of findings
1.2	Compare staffing pattern with standards guidelines	January	Library Media Specialist	None	Chart findings
1.3	Develop a staffing profile for the last 5 yrs.; consider changes in enrollment	February–March	Library Media Specialist	Previous annual reports/Interview key teachers and administrators	Timeline
1.4	Survey teachers regarding their needs: class groups; small groups, individuals	March–May	Library Media Specialist	None	Report results of summary
1.5	Develop a prototype schedule	May	Library Media Specialist	Weekly schedule	Report a summary of the schedule
1.6	Identify periods on schedule when no LMS is available to individual students	End of May	Library Media Specialist	None	Color code period with no professional support.
1.7	Calculate staff requirements to cover the inadequacies (if any)	June 15	Library Media Specialist	None	Document results
1.8	Review findings in light of new school year demands	End of September	Library Media Specialist	Weekly schedule—interview principal to determine changes impacting schedule	Amend report
1.9	Present to budget committee	September–October	Library Media Specialist	None	Evaluate results

PLANNING TEMPLATE 6.1
GOAL REVIEW

Goal statement:

_____

_____

_____

How did this goal assist in fulfilling the library's mission?

_____

_____

_____

To what degree did this goal enable the library to fulfill its roles? Which roles, specifically does this goal address?

_____

_____

_____

To what extent did this goal provide a basis from which library staff could write clear and measurable objectives?

_____

_____

_____

Recommendations for revising this goal statement *(check one)*:
□ Maintain goal as currently written
□ Drop this goal
□ Revise this goal in the following manner:

_____

_____

_____

PLANNING TEMPLATE 6.2
GOALS AND OBJECTIVES

Objective Verbs

establish	initiate
improve	expand
provide	conduct
reduce	decrease
minimize	introduce
increase	develop

Goals Checklist

- Does it describe a priority condition that the library believes is important in fulfilling its roles and mission?

- Is it stated in a declarative sentence?

- Is it free of jargon and easily understood?

- Can the benefit to the user be seen?

- Does it provide a guide for objectives and activities for the next three to five years?

Objectives Checklist

- Does it clearly support the goal?

- Does it include a date by which it must be achieved?

- Does it focus on an end result (what and when)?

- Is it measurable?

Activities Checklist

- Does it provide a series of steps (method) to achieve its end?

- Does it include estimated budget impacts?

- Does it identify who is responsible?

PLANNING TEMPLATE 6.3
OBJECTIVES AND ACTIVITIES ASSESSMENT

Objective # _____

Activities used to accomplish this objective: _____

_____

_____

Were activities completed on schedule: _____ (yes) _____ (no) If no, explain below:

_____

_____

Strengths and weaknesses of the activity(ies): _____

_____

_____

Evidence of the degree to which the objective was accomplished: _____

_____

_____

Factors that contributed to or hindered the accomplishment of the objectives: _____

_____

_____

Recommendations for this objective for the next objectives cycles: _____

_____

_____

_____

Sample Program Goals

Learning and Teaching

Establish collaborative partnerships with teachers to develop effective learning strategies and activities that implement the [state] curriculum standards.

Assist teachers in creating and designing curricula that incorporate information, technology, and media literacy standards across the curriculum.

Provide instruction to teachers and students in information search strategies, evaluation, analysis, and synthesis of information.

Encourage the presentation of information in a variety of formats using current technologies.

Promote individual and collaborative student inquiry by actively engaging students in the learning process and authentic activities.

Assess student achievement of information literacy and technology concepts and processes.

Collaborate with teachers to design learning activities which support inquiry and resource based learning.

Integrate information literacy skills and the district's technology competencies throughout the curriculum for grades _____ through _____.

Teach information literacy and technology skills to foster growth as a critical consumer of information and as an active life-long learner.

Follow information/technology standards established by the school district, state, and national organizations.

Provide instruction to teachers and students in search strategies and the research process for the effective and efficient use of automated and electronic resources.

Provide learning experiences that encourage students to become skilled users and creators of information.

Promote integrated and interdisciplinary learning activities within the school.

Enable students to learn, practice, and transfer information literacy skills taught within the context of classroom learning.

Information Access and Delivery

Develop an inquiry-based environment with flexible scheduling that will promote research, group collaboration, and individual learning.

Devise a collection development plan to support the changes in curriculum resulting from revisions of the state frameworks.

Establish flexible and equitable access to information, ideas, and resources for learning

Develop a quality collection that supports the school's curriculum and meets the diverse learning needs and styles of individual students.

Develop a collection development plan that includes faculty and student participation and reflects the depth and breadth of the curriculum.

Examine the benefits of expanded collaboration with other agencies, e.g. ILL, resource sharing, cooperative purchasing, etc.

Enhance the availability and access to the LMC within and without the school day.

Provide comprehensive reference services, bibliographies, new acquisition alerts, and resource lists for faculty and students.

Promote and ensure intellectual freedom and an atmosphere of free inquiry.

Provide equitable and flexible access to current technologies and diverse information resources.

Assist teachers and students in using educational technologies for information retrieval and presentation methods.

Network with other educational, community and library organizations to expand resource sharing.

Develop and implement, in collaboration with teachers, policies and procedures that maximize access to resources.

Comply with the legal and ethical principles governing intellectual property rights.

Program Administration

Improve resource access and facilitate more efficient management of the program by expanding and reorganizing the facilities.

Provide leadership, collaboration, and assistance to teachers and others in applying principles of instructional design in instruction and the integration of information technology.

Establish an active library media center committee that represents the school community's stakeholders.

Inform staff of changes in curriculum frameworks as quickly as possible.

Develop a comprehensive advocacy program for the LMC.

Coordinate with the technology specialist the use of common space in the LMC to maximize the teaching/learning environment.

Cooperate, collaborate, and resource share with the local public library.

Develop/revise the selection policy and procedures that includes more active participation by faculty and students.

Advocate for sufficient financial support to allow the SLMC to maintain a high quality, up-to-date collection.

Evaluate current staffing to determine how well the LMC meets current needs and its ability to serve projected needs.

Support and implement the vision, mission, and goals of the library media and technology programs.

Review and revise all policies and procedures.

Regularly assess the strengths and weaknesses of the LMC program and give recommendations for enhancements and improvements.

Communicate and advocate for an exemplary LMC program.

Provide ongoing staff development opportunities to maintain professional knowledge.

Develop a program to provide information literacy and technology skills to faculty.

Develop a process to evaluate the effectiveness of the LMC's program of service to the school community.

STEP 7

THE ACTION PLAN

The action plan is a specific set of strategies or activities established to carry out an objective. It provides a vehicle to articulate the means to accomplish your goals through their objectives. It also serves to prioritize the goals, objectives, and activities—to those that are essential as well as able to be completed within a given time frame. It includes the specific tasks that will be done in a logical order, specific timelines, key events, who is responsible, and/or other measures that will determine how and when the objective is realized. The action plan provides a step-by-step guide that measures and documents the school library media center's progress toward its goals. It enables us to identify existing strengths and make them a foundation upon which we can build change. In order to be successful in implementing an action plan, one needs to involve in the planning process as many people as possible who will be affected by the plan.

> - **What key tasks/resources need to be in place?**
> - **What staff needs to be assigned?**
> - **Who is responsible for oversight?**
> - **What is the time frame for accomplishing the objective?**

Backplanning

One technique that may be used to develop the action plan is called "backplanning." It is a reasonably simple device, one that is very familiar to us from our personal lives. It involves determining the end objective—preferably stated in terms of the student. For example, what will students be doing in the library media center that will demonstrate that the objective has been achieved? From this statement, one plans back toward the current situation, identifying the specifics of what has to be in place to achieve the desired results. This often leads to a three- to five-year sequence to achieve the goal. A simple example would be:

Activity	Year 1	Year 2	Year 3	Objective
Provide WWW access	Plan Program	Purchase hardware	Teach WWW search strategies	Students will be efficient searchers on the WWW

Questions that May Help You Focus Your Thoughts

- What materials or resources will be required?
  - Are they new or on-hand?
  - How long will it take to acquire them?
- What hardware, software, and other equipment is required to reliably meet this objective?
- What library staff time will be involved? Teacher time? Administrative time?

- What supplies will be needed?
- What planning time will be required?
- What special knowledge will need to be taught?
- What skills will students need to bring to this new activity?
- Who will take prime responsibility for the organization of the intermediary steps?
- Is there a cost that can be attached to this objective? If yes, what is it?
- Does the facility support this activity?
- If no, can it be rearranged to do so?
- How does this impact other activities already in place?

Budget

Establishing a cost for achieving objectives and ultimately goals is drawn from the requirements of the objective. Every activity within a school has a cost factor associated with it. Staff time costs the organization money in the form of time; resources cost money in the form of space and upkeep. In today's world, costs can come in many forms, such as license fees, annual maintenance contracts, additional electrical power, security considerations, and the like. Some activities (objectives) can extend or expand services already in place, requiring little additional time or resource investment; others can be very costly.

Measures

One must look at both the input measures and output measures to accurately assess whether achievement of an objective has occurred. Input measures would include such information as:

- Collection adequacy
  - In line with state curriculum frameworks
  - In line with district topics and teaching strategies
- Availability and reliability of hardware
- Currency of selection and acquisition policies and procedures
- Access to interlibrary loan, other collections
- Collection organization and classification accuracy
- Staffing patterns (over previous three years)
  - Professional staff
  - Clerical staff
  - Technical staff
- Fiscal support (over previous three years)
  - Per-student expenditures for resources

Output measures, also called performance measures, are twofold: quantitative and qualitative.

- *Quantitative* measures provide a more statistical approach and may include such measures as: circulation statistics, number of reference questions, number of classes using the library in a given period, currency of collection (state guidelines call for 70 percent of the collection being less than ten years old), number of school library media center sponsored special events, meetings, etc.

- *Qualitative* measures look for levels of user satisfaction with various services or activities, level of assistance provided to users, effectiveness of teaching strategies, and numerous attitudes in relation to how well the user's needs are being met.

Measurement

There are several means of gathering information in order to assess progress toward a goal or objective. Some of these are found in comparing information to state standards, accreditation instruments, etc. Other assessments can be made by soliciting information from stakeholders and other users (or nonusers) of the services. This information can be gathered by using carefully constructed surveys or conducting interviews.

You may want to survey or interview students, faculty, administrators, or combinations of these to both chart your course and to expand the involvement of others in the planning and decision-making process. You may need to use either one or the other, and occasionally both surveys and interviews to learn:

- How important particular aspects of your program are
- What their attitudes are on the need for, importance of, or prioritization of essential elements
- The teacher's thoughts on ranking the list of essential elements as to each element's importance, from their point of view
- What the curriculum leaders envision for the future of their discipline
- Which services currently offered should be discontinued and what new ones should be added
- How students feel the arrangement of the facility could be improved
- How/whether students or faculty use other information sources (e.g., the public library, college libraries, etc.)
- How well the teachers and administrators understand the meaning of Information Literacy. (It may be useful to use the AASL Information Literacy Competencies (1995) to determine where teachers and/or administrators are in their basic understanding of the topic.)
- How well the collection meets the needs of the assignments
- Which staff development programs to offer

Some tips and techniques for constructing surveys and interview questions are included in the appendix.

PLANNING TEMPLATE 7.1
ACTION PLAN

Goal #1 _____

_____

	Name	**Brief Description**
Possible Activity 1		
Possible Activity 2		
Possible Activity 3		
Possible Activity 4		

Notes:

_____

_____

_____

STEP 8

ACTION PLAN UPDATES

By October 1 of each year, the action plan should be reviewed and revised to reflect activities that will take place in the next fiscal year to achieve the long-range plan's goals and objectives. This update can be accomplished by a reactivation of the planning committee, or created internally from the measures and documentation of progress within the school. Copies of these updates will need to be attached to all copies of the original document, wherever the copies may reside.

A brief report noting progress toward goals and accomplishments of objectives should accompany the update of goals, objectives, and a revised budget reflecting the changes.

STEP 9

APPROVAL PROCESS

In order to have your long-range plan approved, it will need to be presented to an appropriate governing body. In some schools, that will be the principal, superintendent, or director; in others final approval will rest with school committees or boards of trustees. The protocol for this process would best follow standard school, school district, or private school practice. Whatever route is chosen by your particular institution, the long-range plan needs to be "signed-off" by an appropriate authority.

Governing Board Approval

The signature of the school's principal, superintendent, private school director or headmaster, and/or the school committee or board of trustees indicates that they have reviewed and approved the plan.

Publish and Distribute

Once completed, the long-range plan should be photocopied or printed and distributed. Format it carefully to create an attractive, interesting document that invites reading.

The long-range plan is too important a document to be used for a single purpose. It provides a clear articulation of the library media center program in your district and school for administrators, school committees, boards of trustees, teachers, parents, and the community at large. It also includes the data and information you will need to develop budget requests that can be based on concrete program activities that enable curriculum and learning, respond to an accreditation questionnaire, or used as the foundation for the development of an advocacy program.

Public Relations

The ease of the approval process may depend on your having kept various constituencies informed as the plan evolved. Initiating a public relations program based on the time frame of the plan's development may be sufficient to keep everyone informed. Newsletters, brief faculty meeting announcements, minutes of meetings, brief memos, or invitations to a preliminary (public) presentation are all avenues that should be explored for the most advantageous means at your particular institution. The cultures of organizations differ and will influence how you "get the word out."

STEP 10

EVALUATION

The development of an effective evaluation design is an integral part of the development of a strategic plan. It enables you to gather data on the progress the plan has made and helps one to know what has gone well and what needs to be revised. The evaluation process includes four basic functions:

1. collection of information
2. organization of information
3. analysis of information
4. reporting of information

Evaluation has many definitions. It can mean professional judgment, measurement, assessing performance against specific objectives, or delineating, obtaining, and providing useful information for judging decision alternatives.

When focusing on the evaluation design, first identify the major levels at which the evaluation will be conducted—will it be done school-wide or district-wide? Identify the major evaluative questions to be answered. For each question, you will need to identify the information needed to answer the question. The questions should be developed from the goals and objectives.

Collection of Information. Specify the source of the information to be collected. With whom are you going to work to collect the information? Specify the instruments and methods for collecting the needed information. Will you use a survey? Will you develop a rubric to analyze specific student products for desired characteristics? It is also important to specify how the subjects will be determined. Will you employ a sampling procedure? How will that be determined? Will you use all of the teachers in a specific grade? It is also important to specify the conditions and schedule for information collections. When will this data collection occur? Will it occur during the first month of the plan, during a month in the middle of the plan, and again during a final month of the plan? A schedule needs to be developed so that it is clear exactly when the data will be collected. It is also important to say under what circumstances the data will be collected. Will it be collected during a teachers meeting? Will it be collected when a teacher is in the library media center with his/her class? Will it be collected through a survey placed in teacher's mailboxes?

Organization of Information. A format needs to be determined for working with the information that is to be collected. Once the information is collected, it needs to be put into a format that will enable it to be easily analyzed. For example, will you put the collected information into a database? A database makes it easier to sort, organize, and ask questions. It is also important as a part of the evaluation design to designate a means for coding, organizing, storing, and retrieving information. When one has a clear idea of how to store, sort, and analyze the information, it influences how the collection instruments are developed.

Analysis of Information. Select the analytical procedures to be employed and designate a means for performing the analysis. The analytical procedure could be as simple as determining the average of all of the responses in a particular category. It could mean creating a chart to determine the frequency of responses in each category. It could mean developing percentages of responses in each category and analyzing for the implications. Charts and graphs developed from spreadsheets are also powerful tools to help others interpret the results of a study.

Reporting of Information. To whom will you be presenting your results? It is important to know your audience(s). This can affect how you structure your reporting. Does it need to be very formal or can it be more informal in nature and style? How will you provide the information to the audience or audiences? What format or formats will be most appropriate? Will you publish a formal report? Will you hold a series of informational seminars throughout the district to enable all segments of the community to attend? Will you tape a cable television show for viewing in many different time slots to inform the whole community of the results? Will you just post something on the school Web page? Will you use a combination of all of the above?

The administration of the evaluation includes summarizing the evaluation schedule so that everyone is clear on what will be happening and when it will be happening. Next define staff and resource requirements and plans for meeting these requirements. Carefully look at the evaluation design and determine its potential for providing information, which is valid, reliable, credible, timely, pervasive, and economical. Indicate and schedule means for periodic updating of the evaluation design. Provide a budget for the total evaluation program.

APPENDIX A

COMPETENCIES

Final Report
New England Educational Media Association Task Force to Develop Competencies, Questions for
Evaluators, and Indicators of Quality for the School Library Media Program

The School Library Media Program: Profile and Alignment Document

Criteria and Indicators

1. Information literacy is an integral part of the curriculum
   The evaluator is looking for evidence that the library technology and media program plays a critical role in teaching and learning activities.

   - Information literacy skills are embedded within the curriculum of most disciplines.
   - Teachers and students use the resources of the library media center for teaching and learning.
   - The administration, teachers, students, and community understand and support the learning goals and objectives of the library media program.

2. Collaborative planning and teaching
   The evaluator is looking for evidence of coordination with classroom teachers and the promotion of information literacy skills.

   - Library media specialists participate in building, district, and departmental or grade level curriculum development/assessment on a regular basis.
   - Library media specialists work with teachers as instructional partners in unit development and implementation.

3. Resource-based learning experiences and environments
   - The resource collection is selected and developed cooperatively by the library media specialist and faculty to support the school's curriculum and to contribute to the learning goals of teachers and students.
   - A collection development plan is in place in order to ensure that resources reflect both current and in-depth knowledge.
   - The collection is of sufficient breadth and currency to be pertinent to the school's program of studies.
   - The library media center provides adequate, appropriate space for program resources, services and activities.

4. Use of resources in all formats as a valid, valuable base for learning in all subject areas
   - Learning needs of all students are met through access to information and ideas located in a multi-formatted resource collection that is supported by reliable equipment, and that is also adequate or in sufficient quantity for the student population who utilize the resources.
   - Students are able to demonstrate knowledge in the use of a wide variety of resources and equipment.

5. Use of technology as a tool or resource to facilitate student learning
   - The program provides electronic resources and focuses on the utilization of these resources in the information literacy curriculum of various content areas.
   - Students use technology to foster inquiry and master skills necessary for an information literate, life-long learner.
   - There is evidence, through the student's ability to use technology, to solve information problems.
   - There is evidence that information literacy and technology skills have been linked in content curricula to promote the transfer of information problem solving strategies across all disciplines.

6. Professional growth and development
   - School library media specialists participate in effective staff development to consistently update skills and knowledge—especially as they relate to information literacy issues and related technologies. There is evidence that the library media specialist is aware of effective practices and current research in the area of student learning and information literacy.

7. Management of resources and access
   - The materials of the resource collection are included in a bibliographic control system that uses standardized formats for classification and cataloging.
   - Resources are circulated according to procedures that ensure confidentiality of borrower records and promote free and easy access for students and staff.
   - There is evidence that resources are readily accessible to students and staff because of effective acquisition and circulation policies and procedures, resource sharing, and access to electronic resources outside of the school.
   - The collection is organized for maximum and effective use.
   - A flexible schedule is maintained to ensure access by students and teachers at point of need.

8. Advocacy
   - The program is promoted by school library media personnel who model the importance of information literacy in education, publicize available services and resources to students, staff, and the community, serve on school and district-wide committees, and participate in community projects.
   - There is evidence that the value of the library program to students and staff is well articulated and clearly understood by administration and faculty.

9. Ethical use of ideas and information
   - The program promotes the responsible use of ideas and information through collaboration with teachers, administrators, and others in the development of policies and procedures that comply with current copyright and other laws that pertain to intellectual property.
   - The program actively models the ethical use of information and information technologies in the provision of services relating to the use and/or duplication of resources in any and all formats, confidentiality of records, and equitable access.

Questions/Evidence of Student Learning/Library Program Interaction

1. What evidence exists that teachers understand the interdependence and fundamental relationship between the classroom and the library program to ensure that students are information literate? (1 and 3)
2. In what ways are students able to demonstrate their proficiency in the use of a variety of print, media, and electronic resources to solve information problems and make connections across the curriculum? (4)
3. In what ways are students able to use technology to acquire, organize, evaluate, and present information? (5)
4. What impact/effect has the library staff's professional development had on how students are able to access, evaluate, and present information? (6)
5. Give examples of student, faculty, and community value for the library media and technology program, i.e., financial support, staffing pattern, facilities, and utilization of facility, resources and collection data. (8)
6. What evidence exists that students and others in the school (administration, faculty, and staff) are ethical users of ideas and information as it relates to the library program (for example, copyright, appropriate citation of resources, etc.)? (9)
7. What evidence exists to show that the policies, operation, and organization of the library program support student and faculty needs? For example: Is the circulation policy fair? Can users locate what they need, when they need it? Is there a selection or collection development policy? Are the hours of operation sufficient? (7)
8. What evidence exists that teachers and library media specialists plan in collaboration to benefit student learning? (2)

Level of Collaboration Rubric

1. There is no collaboration beyond scheduling the library.
2. The teacher requests library time and the library media specialist pulls resources for use in the library or classroom.
3. An introduction to resources is provided at the beginning of a unit; resources are pulled and a schedule determined.
4. The library media specialist plans with teachers, offering suggestions and strategies, as well as pulling resources and determining a schedule.
5. Instruction in information literacy skills or concepts is provided as a result of co-planning units or lessons with teachers, as well as the pulling of resources and determining a schedule.

Criteria upon Which Questions/Evidences Are Based

1. Information literacy as an integral part of the curriculum
2. Collaborative planning and teaching
3. Resource-based learning experiences and environments
4. Use of resources in all formats as a valid and valuable base for learning in all subject areas
5. Use of technology as a tool or resource to facilitate student learning
6. Professional growth and development
7. Management of resources and access
8. Advocacy

APPENDIX B

SCHOOL LIBRARY MEDIA CENTER DEVELOPMENT PLAN

(School Library Media Center Name)
(School District)
(Date)

Part I. Introduction to the Planning Process

This long-range plan was produced using the *School Library Media Center Long-Range Planning Guide*, a planning guide for school library media centers. The purpose of the planning process is to help school libraries identify and analyze their school community and program needs, determine key library service activities and roles, and develop goals and objectives which will help the school library media center carry out its mission and support the mission of the school.

The _____ school library media center has undertaken the planning process for the following reasons:

_____

_____

_____

A committee (provide a list of committee members) under the leadership of _____ developed this plan. The library media specialists served as primary resource persons, gathering and analyzing data, identifying library needs, crafting survey instruments to facilitate data gathering from a wide range of interested parties, and developing assessment methods. Planning committee members assisted in sharing the work of this task.

The plan produced by this process will serve as a framework that will guide school library media center development in the schools for the next three to five years. The plan will not be static. It will be reviewed and revised each year to keep pace with the success of progress as old objectives are met and new ones evolve.

Contents of this plan include:

- Description of plan's methodology and development
- Community description
- Mission statement (vision statement is optional)
- Library needs assessment

- Facility, staffing, program, and resources
- Goals and objectives
- Action plan [future years, an update]
- Approval

Summary Planning Guide

School Library Media Center Long-Range Planning Guide

Planning: What Is It?

Planning is a process having to do with determining where you want to go, where you are now, and ways to get from here to there. Planning enables you to reflect upon where you are now, then think about and do something about the future. Effective planning enables you to make decisions about the key components of your practice. It helps you articulate your vision and facilitates your identifying the steps you need to take to be able to arrive at your vision. In order for one to be successful in implementing an action plan, one needs to involve in the planning process as many people as possible who will be affected by the plan.

> **Plans must include the following elements:**
>
> - **Brief description of plan's development and methodology**
> - **Community scan**
> - **Mission statement (vision statement is optional)**
> - **Current status (needs assessment)**
> - **Multiyear goals and objectives**
> - **Action plan (Year 1) with measures to determine progress**
> - **Governing body approval**
> - **Action plan updates (subsequent years)**

The purpose of the long-range plan is to give you the opportunity to conceptualize and describe the significant goals you wish to achieve in your school library media program within the next one to five years and to plan how to achieve these goals.

The plan must include the following components:

A. Description of Your School Community: Describe your school community. Include in your description any special programs within the school and any groups with any special needs that your school serves. Please try to include the elements that make your school unique.

B. Description of Library Media Program: Describe your library media program as it currently exists. Be sure to include any special programs, e.g., Electronic Bookshelf, Accelerated Reader, or assistive technology. Describe your library access schedule, involvement with flexible scheduling, outreach to classes, cooperative teaching, curriculum development, integration of technology, involvement with the reading program and literacy development, and the budget for the school library media center.

C. Vision (Optional): A vision statement is a set of words or precepts you can put together so that you are focusing on a distantly achievable goal. What is your vision of what the library media program could be in your school? As a result of the completion of this long-range plan, how will your situation be different three to five years from now? What will teachers/staff members be saying or doing differently? What will students be saying or doing differently?

D. Mission Statement: The mission statement represents the school library media center's reason for being. A good mission statement should accurately explain why your school library media center exists and what it hopes to achieve in the future. It articulates the organization's essential nature, its values, and its work. It should be free of jargon. The mission statement should answer the following questions:

1. What are the opportunities or needs that we exist to address? (The purpose of the organization.)
2. What are we doing to address these needs? (The business of the organization.)
3. What principles or beliefs guide our work? (The values of the organization.)

Make a worksheet based on these questions. Ask staff, teachers, volunteers, students, etc., to list any words, phrases, or ideas that come to mind with respect to the library media center and these various questions. Give everyone a chance to be heard. Look for language and concepts that enjoy great repetition.

E. Needs Statement: Where are you now? What is it you need to go from where you are now to the realization of the vision? What resources already exist within the school department, or outside agency resources that are, or can be devoted to the implementation of the proposed program? What additional resources are needed (funding, personnel, equipment, space, etc.) to make the vision a reality? You should include initial, one-time, and ongoing costs for operating the program or implementing the change. What are the needs relative to technology? What are the needs of the library media center with regard to the Americans with Disabilities Act? What are the barriers? Outline corrective action. Prioritize.

F. Multiyear Goals and Objectives: Goals are broad statements describing desirable ends toward which the library media center will work over the long-term, encompassing a vision of what services should be available. A goal is not measurable and may never be fully reached, but will probably not change over a three- to five-year period. Together with objectives, goals define a course of action for meeting the needs of a school community. Objectives are specific short-range statements of results to be achieved to implement a goal. They define how it will be done, who will do it, and when and under what conditions. Objectives are measurable, include time frames and may or may not change over a three- to five-year period depending upon progress made.

G. Action Plan: For at least the first year of the multiyear goals and objectives develop an action plan that includes activities, with specific time frames and/or other means for measuring progress, for achieving the objectives. The action plan enables you to articulate the means to be used to accomplish an objective including specific tasks that will be done in a given year to achieve that objective; activities should include specific timelines and/or other measures for determining when the activities will take place and how the objective will be accomplished. Indicate what is to be done and by whom, when, how, and with what resources.

H. Brief Description of Plan's Methodology: Here identify the specific planning process used—if you are using the process outlined in this planning document.

I. Approval of Governing Board: The signatures of the committee chair, school principal, district superintendent, headmaster, and/or the chair of the school committee or board of trustees indicates that they have reviewed and approved the plan.

J. Annual Update of Action Plans: By October 1 of each year, the action plan should be reviewed and revised to reflect activities that will take place in the next fiscal year to achieve the long-range plan's goals and objectives.

Things to Consider and Answer before You Begin to Complete the Template

1. Have you read *Information Power: Building Partnerships for Learning*? What did you learn from it to help you in thinking about your program? How can it help you to educate your school community about the modern role of the library media program?

2. Have you visited some exemplary school library media programs to explore what your school community might be able to replicate?

3. What services might you be able to initiate to help increase basic literacy?

4. Are information literacy skills embedded within the curricula of most disciplines in your school?

5. What is the condition of your collection? What needs to be done to improve it?

6. Is the faculty involved with the library media specialist in collection development?

7. Is there a collection development plan in place?

8. Is the collection of sufficient breadth and currency to be pertinent to the school's program of studies?

9. Is the library media center involved with the storage and circulation of computer software?

10. Is the library media center involved in the record keeping required for computer software site licensing?

11. Has the school library media center been able to develop multicultural resources? If not, should that be a priority now?

12. Has your school library media center been automated? How could automation enhance your school library media program?

13. Where is the library media center's involvement with technology? What electronic resources are available for students and staff? Is the Internet available? How is access obtained? Are teachers and students learning how to access efficiently and effectively the information from electronic resources? What electronic library resources are available throughout the whole school? What are your equipment, electronic database, and software needs?

14. Is technology seen as a vital tool for information problem solving?

15. What are your space needs?

16. What are your renovation needs?

17. What are your furniture needs?

18. What are the staff development/training needs of the school library media specialist, library staff, teachers and the principal?

19. How is school release time currently used? Could it be used to help facilitate staff development in the access and use of information via the resources available in the library media center?

20. What is the level of parental involvement? Could parents be tapped to help with some of the needs of the school library media center?

21. Would the services of a consultant be useful in helping to educate the school community to the needs of the library media center program?

22. What are the staffing requirements and personnel needs to be able to carry out the tasks required by the type of program envisioned?

23. Has the library media specialist been involved in curriculum planning? If not, how could the library media specialist become involved?

24. What role can the library media program play in the implementation of the state's curriculum frameworks?

25. Who should be involved in your school library media center long-range planning? How do you get them involved?

26. Do you have community businesses that could be involved? How could you get them involved?

27. Do you have an effective library media program advocacy program? What would you need to do to put one in place?

TEMPLATE

This summary template, a compilation of forms distributed throughout the guidelines, provides a framework for a long-range plan. Answers to the questions and information items contained below are to be woven into a seamless narrative that would constitute the long-range plan.

A. Description of Your School Community

Answering the following questions will help you to develop your school library media center school community description.

1. Brief description of the city or town the school is in. This gives the picture of the broader school community. Information for this can be extracted from WWW department of education sites as well as local educational sites.

_____

_____

_____

_____

2. How many children attend your school? _____

3. What grade levels does your school serve? _____

4. Please describe both your town and your school community. Include demographics, such as population, location, total area, race and ethnicity, income distribution, educational level of the community, money per pupil for schools, etc.

_____

_____

_____

_____

5. Any special programs in the school?

_____

_____

_____

6. Any special-needs programs?

_____

_____

_____

7. What makes your school unique? For example, does it have a special mission, special populations, etc.?

_____

_____

_____

_____

8. Provide a brief summary of the results of state testing and the impact on the school library media center program.

_____

_____

_____

B. Description of the Library Media Program

1. Briefly describe your library media program as it currently exists.

_____

_____

_____

2. What special programs does your library media center provide?

_____

_____

_____

_____

3. How do students get access to the library media center?

_____

_____

_____

_____

4. How do teachers access the services of the library media center and of the library media specialist?

_____

_____

_____

_____

5. Are you working on developing a flexibly accessed library media program? If yes, how?

_____

_____

_____

6. Is the library media specialist involved in cooperative planning with the classroom teachers?

_____

_____

_____

_____

7. Is the library media specialist involved in curriculum development with the classroom teachers?

_____

_____

_____

8. Describe how technology is integrated into the library media program.

_____

_____

_____

_____

9. Describe library media center involvement with the reading program and literacy development in the school.

_____

_____

_____

10. What is the budget for the school library media center? (Include breakdown by categories.)

_____

_____

_____

_____

C. Mission Statement

Answering the following questions will help you to develop your school library media center mission statement.

1. What are the opportunities or needs that the school library media center exists to address?

_____

_____

_____

2. What are we doing to address these needs?

_____

_____

_____

3. What principles or beliefs guide our work?

_____

_____

_____

_____

4. Make a worksheet based on the above questions and ask staff, teachers, volunteers, students, etc., to list any words, phrases, or ideas that come to mind with respect to the library media center and these various questions. Look for language and concepts that enjoy great repetition. Use this area to summarize the comments made.

_____

_____

_____

_____

_____

_____

_____

5. Based on the above responses, use the space below to write your mission statement.

_____

_____

_____

_____

_____

D. Vision

A vision statement is a set of words or precepts you can put together so you are focusing on a distantly achievable goal. Answering the following questions will help you to develop your school library media center vision statement.

1. What is your vision of what the library media program could be in your school? As a result of the completion of this long-range plan, how will your situation be different three to five years from now?

_____

_____

_____

_____

2. What will teachers/staff members be saying or doing differently?

_____

_____

_____

_____

_____

3. What will students be saying or doing differently?

_____

_____

_____

_____

_____

4. Based on the above responses, use the space below to write your vision statement.

_____

_____

_____

_____

_____

E. Needs Statement

Answering the following questions will help you to develop your school library media center needs statement.

1. What are your program needs to go from where you are now to the realization of the vision? (Note: This is not what hardware, staff, or other "things" you think you want or need—but what enhancements to your program would get you closer to your goals.)

_____

_____

_____

_____

2. What resources already exist within the school department or outside agency resources that are, or can be, devoted to the implementation of the proposed program?

_____

_____

_____

_____

3. What additional resources are needed (print, non-print resources including electronic resources, personnel, equipment, space, etc.) to make the vision a reality? You should include initial, one-time, and ongoing costs for operating the program or implementing the change.

_____

_____

_____

_____

4. What are the needs relative to technology?

_____

_____

_____

5. What is the impact on existing/future staff needs?

_____

_____

_____

_____

6. What are the needs of the library media center with regard to the Americans with Disabilities Act? What are the barriers? Outline corrective action.

_____

_____

_____

_____

7. Use the space below to prioritize the responses to 1 through 7 above.

_____

_____

_____

_____

_____

F. Multiyear Goals and Objectives

Goals: Broad statements describing desirable end results toward which the library media center will work over the long-term, encompassing a vision of what services should be available. A goal is not measurable and may never be fully reached but will probably not change over a three- to five-year period. Together with objectives, goals define a course of action for meeting the needs of a school community.

Based on the information gathered in the previous sections, please list three goals for your library media center.

_____

_____

_____

_____

Objectives: Specific, short-range statements of results to be achieved to implement a goal. They define what will be done and when. Objectives are measurable, often in terms of student behavior or demonstrated abilities. They include time frames, and may or may not change over a three- to five-year period depending on progress made. Based on the goals listed in the section above, develop the objectives needed to fulfill each goal in the spaces provided below.

_____

_____

_____

_____

_____

_____

_____

_____

_____

_____

_____

_____

G. Action Plan: For at least the first year of the multiyear goals and objectives, develop an action plan that includes activities, with specific time-frames and/or other means for measuring progress, for achieving the objectives. The action plan enables you to articulate the means to be used to accomplish an objective including specific tasks that will be done in a given year to achieve that objective. Activities should include specific timelines and/or other measures for determining when the activities will take place and how the objective will be accomplished. This is the detailed step-by-step plan that leads to the achievement of an objective. Indicate what is to be done, by whom, when, and with what resources.

On the following pages outline your action plan.

Action Plan

The purpose of the action plan is to give you the opportunity to conceptualize and describe the significant goals you wish to achieve in your school library media program within the first year, and to plan how to achieve these goals.

Goal 1

_____

_____

_____

_____

Objectives Linked to Goal 1

Goal 1. Objective 1 (For year one)

_____

_____

_____

_____

Activities for Objective 1: Below write activities for each objective and establish timelines or dates for the accomplishment of each step.

_____

_____

_____

_____

Assessment and Documentation for Objective 1: Indicate below how you will assess and document implementation of objectives and activities.

_____

_____

_____

_____

Goal 1. Objective 2 (For year one)

_____

_____

_____

_____

Activities for Objective 2: Below write activities for each objective and establish timelines or dates for the accomplishment of each step.

_____

_____

_____

_____

_____

_____

Assessment and Documentation for Objective 2: Indicate below how you will assess and document implementation of objectives and activities.

_____

_____

_____

_____

Goal 1. Objective 3 (For year one)

_____

_____

_____

_____

Activities for Objective 3: Below write activities for each objective and establish timelines or dates for the accomplishment of each step.

_____

_____

_____

_____

_____

Assessment and Documentation for Objective 3: Indicate below how you will assess and document implementation of objectives and activities.

_____

_____

_____

_____

Goal 2

_____

_____

_____

_____

Objectives Linked to Goal 2

Goal 2. Objective 1 (For year one)

_____

_____

_____

_____

Activities for Objective 1: Below write activities for each objective and establish timelines or dates for the accomplishment of each step.

_____

_____

_____

_____

Assessment and Documentation for Objective 1: Indicate below how you will assess and document implementation of objectives and activities.

_____

_____

_____

_____

Goal 2. Objective 2 (For year one)

_____

_____

_____

_____

Activities for Objective 2: Below write activities for each objective and establish timelines or dates for the accomplishment of each step.

_____

_____

_____

_____

Assessment and Documentation for Objective 2: Indicate below how you will assess and document implementation of objectives and activities.

_____

_____

_____

_____

Goal 2. Objective 3 (For year one)

_____

_____

_____

_____

Activities for Objective 3: Below write activities for each objective and establish timelines or dates for the accomplishment of each step.

_____

_____

_____

_____

_____

_____

_____

_____

_____

_____

Assessment and Documentation for Objective 3: Indicate below how you will assess and document implementation of objectives and activities.

_____

_____

_____

Goal 3

_____

_____

_____

_____

Objectives Linked to Goal 3

Goal 3. Objective 1 (For year one)

_____

_____

_____

_____

Activities for Objective 1: Below write activities for each objective and establish timelines or dates for the accomplishment of each step.

_____

_____

_____

_____

_____

_____

_____

Assessment and Documentation for Objective 1: Indicate below how you will assess and document implementation of objectives and activities.

_____

_____

_____

_____

Goal 3. Objective 2 (For year one)

_____

_____

_____

_____

Activities for Objective 2: Below write activities for each objective and establish timelines or dates for the accomplishment of each step.

_____

_____

_____

_____

_____

_____

_____

Assessment and Documentation for Objective 2: Indicate below how you will assess and document implementation of objectives and activities.

_____

_____

_____

_____

Goal 3. Objective 3 (For year one)

_____

_____

_____

_____

Activities for Objective 3: Below write activities for each objective and establish timelines or dates for the accomplishment of each step.

_____

_____

_____

Assessment and Documentation for Objective 3: Indicate below how you will assess and document implementation of objectives and activities.

_____

_____

_____

_____

Plan's Methodology: *School Library Media Center Long-Range Planning Guide* procedures were followed.

List of Committee Members:

Name	Title
Name	Title
Name	Title
Name	Title
Name	Title
Name	Title

_____   _____
Signature(s) of Library Coordinator and/or Committee Chairperson   Date

Approval of Governing Board:

_____   _____   _____   _____
Signature of Superintendent,   Name of School District   Address   Date
Principal, or Director   or Private School

and/or

_____   _____   _____   _____
Signature of School Board   Name of School District   Address   Date
or Board of Trustees Chair   or Private School

APPENDIX C

SURVEY TIPS

Constructing good surveys is not a matter of luck. Poor surveys provide poor information, or at best, information that must be massaged into something meaningful. This introduces a great deal of bias into the responses, and nullifies the findings. To avoid this, the following tips are offered.

Written Surveys

- Ask only questions that really need to be answered. Avoid inserting a question because it "might be interesting to know" but is not seminal to the data you are seeking.
- Always pilot your survey instrument with (first) a few friends or colleagues and if major changes are suggested, re-pilot with a small group of potential responders.
- Keep the language of the question or statement simple. Avoid the use of library jargon. And, remember the age and vocabulary level of the students you are surveying. Youngest children do better with interview-type surveys.
- Select respondents from a sample of individuals who you know will have meaningful input. Surveying people who "don't know" can be useful, for example, when trying to find out why teachers or students don't use the library media center or your services since they are the participants; but under normal circumstances, either a random sample or a stratified sample will provide better information.
- If the respondent group is large (over 50), choose a "workable" sample size and use an appropriate sampling technique.

  - A **random sample** is the equivalent of picking names out of a hat. You could sample certain departments, or groups (freshmen, seniors), but you would select names from a list by (a) generating a list of random numbers and matching the numbers with numbers of the names on the list; or, (b) you could select every fifth or tenth name.
  - A **stratified random sample** involves selecting a subgroup of the whole and applying random sampling techniques just to this group. For example, if you want to find out attitudes of teachers to determine whether you want to continue a particular service, you might want to exclude new teachers from the group. Another example is to select two or three members from each department rather than the whole faculty or an overall random sample of the faculty to respond. This assures all departments are represented. Or, you might want to compare the thoughts of a group of library media center heavy-users to a group of non-users and stratify your sample along these lines.
  - A **weighed random** or **stratified sample** involves the above, but you weight each department based on its size, influence, participation, etc. For example, if the English Department has twelve teachers and the Art Department has three, you might want more representation from the English Department

and you would assign weights to each group and select numbers based on those weights. In this case, the English Department may have four respondents while the Art Department has one.

- Keep the survey as brief as possible—one side of one page, not too many questions, etc.
- Write a *brief* but persuasive cover paragraph or letter succinctly explaining why you need this information and why you think the respondent has the answers you need.
- Allow sufficient time for returns.
- Follow up with either a personal visit or a phone call to nonrespondents.
- If you use ratings, be sure they are consistent and in the same order for each question. For example, Yes/No (in that order); 1–4 (poor to excellent)
- When using a Likert-type scale (1 = poor, 2 = fair, 3 = okay, 4 = good, 5 = excellent, or 1 = N/A, 2 = disagree, 3 = agree, 4 = strongly agree, 5 = complete agreement) plan to use at least five (5) points. If you want finer discrimination, use seven (7) points. It is normally advisable not to use less than three, or more than seven, points.
- Be sure to clearly anchor numbered scales, for example,

    Minimal 1 — 2 — 3 — 4 — 5 Extensive

or

1	2	3	4	5
N/A	Poor	Fair	Good	Excellent

- Be sure to clearly explain what you want the respondent to do. For example, check a box, initial the correct level, and/or circle the number.
- Use surveys sparingly, particularly if you are asking the same group of people.
- Be sure to share the results of the survey with the participants. The data gathered can provide a basis for a public relations announcement.

Interview Surveys

Interviewing is another excellent survey technique, but it has additional techniques. Here are some that might help:

- Carefully craft the questions. Avoid jargon or leading questions that will "get the answer you want to hear."
- Arrange the interview in advance.
- Practice recording the answers for listening to again later.
- Actively listen to the response while refraining from comments, facial expressions, or other body language that, again, can skew the response.
- Safeguard against interviewer bias. You want to hear "their" story, not a reaffirmation of your thoughts.
- Take complete notes and use a recorder if possible.
- Assure the respondent anonymity.
- Pilot the interview with a few individuals.

APPENDIX D

POWERPOINT PRESENTATIONS

Evaluation: How to Formulate an Effective Design

Functions in the Evaluation Process

Usually, evaluations include four functions:

- **Collection** of information
- **Organization** of information
- **Analysis** of information
- **Reporting** of information

Definitions of Evaluation

Evaluation—Professional judgment
Evaluation—Measurement
Evaluation—Assessing performance against specific objectives
Evaluation—Delineating, obtaining, and providing useful information for judging decision alternatives

Definitions of Evaluation

Evaluation: Determination of the worth of a thing. It includes obtaining information to judge the worth of an educational program, product, or procedure, or the potential utility of alternative approaches designed to attain specified objectives.

Developing Evaluation Designs

- Focus the evaluation
- Collect the information
- Organize the information
- Analyze the information
- Report the information
- Administer the evaluation

Focus the Evaluation

- Define policies within which the evaluation must operate.
- Identify the major level(s) at which the evaluation will be conducted, (e.g., national, regional, state, or local).
- Identify the specific program or curriculum that will be evaluated (e.g., district-wide K–6 reading program; athletic program of a particular high school).
- Identify the major evaluative questions to be answered
- For each question, identify information needed to answer the question.

Collect Information

- Specify the **source** of the information to be collected.
- Specify the **instruments and methods** for collecting the needed information.
- Specify the **sampling procedure** to be employed.
- Specify the **conditions and schedule** for information collection.

Organize the Information

- Provide a **format** for the information which is to be collected.
- Designate a **means for coding, organizing, storing, and retrieving the information.**

Analyze the Information

- Select the analytical **procedures** to be employed.
- Designate a **means** for performing the analysis.

Report the Information

- **Define the audiences** for the evaluation reports.
- **Specify means** for providing information to the audiences.
- **Specify the format** for evaluation reports and/or reporting sessions.
- **Schedule** the reporting of information.

Administer the Evaluation

- Summarize the **evaluation schedule**.
- Define **staff** and **resource requirements** and plans for meeting these requirements.
- Specify **means** for **meeting policy requirements** for conduct of the evaluation.
- **Evaluate** the potential of the **evaluation design** for providing information which is valid, reliable, credible, timely, pervasive, and economical.
- Specify and schedule **means for periodic updating** of the evaluation design.
- Provide a **budget** for the total evaluation program.

Long-Range Planning Seminar

Introduction

How did this come about?
Why choose to plan now?

Planning Guide Organization

Text
Overview
Steps to Planning
Planning Template
Appendices

Overview

- Chart the course
- Benefits and characteristics
- Who should plan?
  - School districts
  - Private schools
  - Individual schools

What is a Long-Range Plan?

Strategic planning
- Sets the tone
- Defines primary role
- Informs staff

Operational planning
- Sets goals
- Sets objectives
- Defines key activities

The Cyclical Process

- Planning to Plan
- Current Status and Data Gathering
- Vision and Mission Statements
- Goals and Objectives
- Action Planning
- Evaluation

Steps to Planning—1

Planning to plan
- Why plan
- What support I can develop?
- Who leads?
- Who is involved?
- How large a committee?
- How complex?
- How to keep others informed?
- Cost: time and money

Steps to Planning—2

Connect to the school's mission and setting
- Local school & district documents
- State documents
- Accreditation documents
- National documents

Steps to Planning—3

The Vision Statement
- Developing the "global" perspective

Steps to Planning—4

Essential elements and current status
- Teaching and learning
- Information access and delivery
- Program administration

How Do We Measure Up?

Assessment rubrics
- Understanding
- Frequency
- Effectiveness
- Independence
- Consistency
- Targets for improvement

Steps to Planning—5

The Mission Statement
- Why does the SLMC program exist?
- What opportunities can we address?

- How are we addressing them?
- What principles or beliefs guide our efforts?

Steps to Planning—6

Goals
- Where do you want to go?
- What will be happening?

Objectives
- What steps are needed?
- What activities need to be in place?
- How will they be measured?

Steps to Planning—7

Action Plan
- What key resources and tasks need to be in place?
- What staff needs to be assigned?
- Who is responsible for oversight?
- What is the time frame for accomplishment?

Budget

Steps to Planning—8

Action plan updates
- What has been accomplished?
- What has changed?
- What new directions are indicated?

New budgets

New measures

Steps to Planning—9

Approvals
- Governing body
- Administrators

Appreciation
- Participants
- Stakeholders
- Administrators
- Public at large

Steps to Planning—10

Evaluation
- How has our plan worked?
- What progress have we made on goals and objectives?
- What modifications are needed?
- How is our community informed of our progress and upcoming changes?
- What is our new action plan for next year?

Long-Range Plan Summary

- Brief description of how you planned
- Community scan and demographics
- Vision and Mission Statements
- Current status—Needs assessment
- 3–5 year goals and objectives
- Action plan—Year 1:
  - Activities
  - Time frame
  - Who is responsible?
- Approval
- Evaluation process/evaluation

Investment for the Future

Regardless of the time and effort required,
> planning is the *only* path that leads to . . .
> **PROGRESS**

> All other paths lead *only* to movement.

> "Even if you are on the right track,
> you'll get run over if you just sit there."
> —Will Rogers

APPENDIX E

SAMPLE DISTRICT PLAN

BENNET GROVE PUBLIC SCHOOLS, BENNET GROVE, ILLINOIS
K–12 SCHOOL LIBRARY MEDIA CENTER LONG-RANGE PLAN

Description of Individual Schools

SCHOOL	GRADES	ENROLLMENT
Clear Brook Elementary	K–6	630
Stacey's Corner Elementary	K–6	520
Sutter's Mill Elementary School	K–6	678
Bennet Grove Memorial Junior/Senior High School	7–12	1,087

Description of Community

Bennet Grove

Bennet Grove is a moderate sized residential community situated on the southwestern semi-rural fringe of metropolitan Chicago. Although settled since the colonial era, the town has never experienced any prolonged periods of intensive industrial or commercial development. Bennet Grove evolved from agricultural village to rural small town and to bedroom suburb and now to a major commercial zone. This recent pattern of unbalanced growth is affecting the schools as well as the town in general. In addition, the closing of a private parochial elementary school in town has resulted in a modest influx of students in the lower grades.

The dramatic upsurge in commercial activity in Bennet Grove is a consequence of many factors. The recent influx of ethnic and racial minorities and a large "trade-free" zone are accompanied by rather sudden problems of land shortages, rising prices and congestion. It has, however, allowed Bennet Grove to improve both its business center and upgrade municipal services and public infrastructure—all within a short period of time. The town is also attracting able and committed developers. Unlike the past, Bennet Grove is now prepared for and strongly interested in economic growth.

Bennet Grove also has a strong commitment to providing good municipal services. This commitment is best typified by the recent construction of a new library, fire station, and elementary school, as well as recent improvements in the town's playgrounds and ball fields. But growth has also created enormous pressures on the curriculum within the schools as the population of the town has changed dramatically and the previous shoestring budgeting has seen a sudden and substantial influx of a tax windfall.

Grades/Schools

	Grade Span	Number of Schools
Total	N–12	6
Elementary	N–6	4
Middle/Junior High		
High School	7–12	2
Other		

Enrollment and Staff

Enrollment by Grade

	K	1	2	3	4	5	6	7	8	9	10	11	12	Total
1999–2000	286	267	240	222	205	191	172	158	162	160	153	151	154	2525
2000–2001	315	309	279	256	230	232	207	184	192	222	170	159	160	2915

Race/Ethnicity, 2000–2001

	District	State
African American	9.4	8.6
Asian	2.0	1.2
Hispanic	3.4	1.0
Native American	0.9	0.7
White	84.3	88.5

Selected Populations, 2000–2001

	District	State
Special Education	20.0	16.6
Limited English proficient	7.8	4.7
Eligible for free/reduced-price lunch	18.8	25.8

Staff, 2000–2001 (FTE)

	District	State
Number of students per teacher (Not average class size)	19.6	18.0

Children Attending Public Schools (percent)

District		State	
1996–1997	2000–2001	1996–1997	2000–2001
94.0	97.1	89.2	90.0

Special Programs in the Schools

SCHOOL	PROGRAM
Clear Brook Elementary	Reading Recovery
	Arts Week
	D.A.R.E.
	Reading Partners
	Firefighter Phil
Stacey's Corner Elementary	Reading Recovery
	Title I
	D.A.R.E.
	Firefighter Phil
	RIF
Sutter's Mill Elementary	Title I
	Reading Recovery
	D.A.R.E.
	Grandparent Reading Partners
	Firefighter Phil
	Reading Week
Bennet Grove Memorial Junior/Senior High School	D.A.R.E.
	SADD
	Sexual Harassment
	Peer Leaders
	DECA
	International Festival

Uniqueness of Each School

Clear Brook Elementary School

Our mission is to provide every student with an opportunity to receive the highest quality of education within a stimulating atmosphere in which to learn, and a nurturing environment in which to grow, with respect for each other and self. To accomplish this mission, the following goals have been set forth:

- Update teaching materials and acquire complementary technological equipment
- Provide cultural and enrichment programs that enhance the curriculum
- Integrate the Arts into a variety of subject areas

- Utilize other resources within the Bennet Grove community in the educational process
- Encourage classroom location, space allotment, and time usage with the best interests of the children in mind.
- Foster a climate in which our children will learn respect for all people

Stacey's Corner Elementary

The mission of the Stacey's Corner Elementary School is to prepare students to become knowledgeable citizens who contribute to an ever-changing society by providing its students with an outstanding education driven by a dynamic curriculum, a dedicated staff and a committed community striving for excellence.

Sutter's Mill Elementary School

The Sutter's Mill Elementary School community believes that we are all citizens of one world. In supporting that belief, the staff, students, parents and administration will acknowledge the differences that make us diverse and the similarities that make us one. By working together and encouraging acceptance of individual differences, effective learning will take place in accordance with the philosophy of the Bennet Grove Elementary Schools, which states:

The Learner

We believe that children vary considerably in the areas of physical, cognitive and social/emotional development. Children learn at different rates and in a variety of ways: relying on or favoring one or more sensory modalities (visual, auditory, tactile, etc.).

Children learn through exposure, discussion, experience, modeling, exploration and meaningful practice. Rote learning (memorization) is a major strategy for the mastery of certain basic mathematical skills. Students should be aware of the relevancy of the subject matter; that the material being presented is to develop valuable skills that will be used and further developed throughout their lives. Educational experiences should be successful and positive in order to build student confidence, self-esteem, natural curiosity, a desire to learn, and respect and appreciation for individual differences.

The Learning Process

We believe that students should be engaged in active "hands-on" learning experiences to better assimilate new skills and knowledge. Children need a nurturing environment replete with appropriate instructional materials that provides opportunities for observing, experimenting, discussing and drawing conclusions.

At the core of our philosophy is the belief that a student's attitude toward problem solving is extremely important and that, as teachers, we need to offer each child many opportunities to apply critical thinking skills to successfully address these problems. Students should be involved in the decision-making process.

Curriculum objectives can be met through a medley of teaching strategies. Individual teaching and learning styles are decisive factors for success in all educational areas. Observation and discussion with both peer and adult role models should be part of every learning experience.

We believe that Art, Music, and Physical Education are integral to the core learning experiences of all young people. When understood (appreciated) fully and employed meaningfully, the arts are crucial to helping teachers and students make connections between imagination and learning, between thinking and feeling, between self and environment and between individual and society.

Bennet Grove Memorial Junior/Senior High School

Bennet Grove High School, in partnership with parents and the community, recognizes that learning is a lifelong process requiring a variety of education experiences, resources, and expectations to provide students with opportunities to develop intellectually, socially, physically, and emotionally. In this ever-changing world, we are advocates for active and cooperative learning, respect for self and others, and effective communication and analytical skills. With a goal of confident interaction in a diverse society, each student is challenged to actively participate in school and in the community, to assume responsibility for setting and achieving personal goals, and to learn skills requisite for productive contribution to society.

Description of the Elementary Library Media Program

- Vision Statement

The Bennet Grove Public Schools Library Media Program provides all students with a viable library media program integrated with the curriculum. With the cooperation of the staff, the library media program will enable students to find, evaluate, and use information. As a result of the library media program, the students will become independent, productive, lifelong learners who will enhance and contribute to the community.

- Mission Statement

The Bennet Grove Public Schools Library Media Program will enable students to become independent learners by stimulating a love of reading and learning.

- Current Status
  - All classes 1–6 receive a 45-minute library period once a week.
  - All kindergarten students receive a 30-minute library period once a week.
  - All receive a weekly story time in grades K–3.
  - All receive library skills instruction according to the students' ability level in grades K–6.
  - All receive instruction in how to use the computer as a reference tool.
  - All assist with specialized reading programs in their schools.
  - All purchase materials to support the K–6 curriculum.
  - All manage all audiovisual equipment and accompanying resources. This item includes inventorying, minor repairs and lamp replacement.
  - Two of the school library media centers run parent volunteer programs.
  - Two of the school library media programs sponsor library media center fundraisers.

- Elementary Library Media Center Goals and Objectives

  Goal 1: There will be adequate resources available in the library media center to meet the resource needs of the Illinois Curriculum guidelines.

  Objectives:
      1.1   Examine each collection for alignment with the Illinois curriculum guidelines
      1.2   Establish a collection development plan
      1.3   Implement plan

  Goal 2: Utilize library media center staff to enable continuous growth and program development.

Objectives:
2.1   Provide time for planning for future program development.
2.2   Provide staff development opportunities tied directly to library program needs including attendance at appropriate conferences.
2.3   Fulfill vision of the library media program through the development of a plan for the hiring of a certified elementary school library media specialist.

Goal 3: All libraries in the community will be networked through a uniform automation system.

Objectives:
3.1   Work with the public library director, the high school library media specialist, the director of technology, and the system's administration to develop a plan for automation in all schools, K–12.

Goal 4: Develop a written library media curriculum framework, which integrates information problem solving into the total curricula of the school system.

Objectives:
4.1   Form a library media curriculum writing committee.
4.2   Examine exemplary library media curriculum documents from other school systems.
4.3   Establish what the Bennet Grove Public School children need to know and be able to do upon completion of grades 6, 8, and 12.

Goal 5: To foster a love of reading in the community, develop a cooperatively planned and implemented summer reading program.

Objectives:
5.1   The director of curriculum will call a meeting with the principals K–12, the library media specialists and assistants, representative teachers, and the director of the public library to formulate a plan to develop the summer reading program.

Memorial Junior/Senior High School

Current Status—Strengths
The following strengths of the Memorial Junior/Senior High School Library Media Program are cited in the accreditation report dated April 30, 1999:

1. The librarian's efforts to deliver services with no support staff and with limited resources.
2. The ability of the librarian and audiovisual director to coordinate with the faculty.
3. The library is open two afternoons after school.
4. The close working relationship between the public library and school librarian.
5. The students' support of the library's organization and the librarian's ability to assist them.
6. The five new computers with Internet access and one printer, which have been recently added to the library.

Current Status—Needs
The results of the accreditation self-study and the visiting team reports specify the following recommendations:

1. Provide adequate level of professional staff to ensure the effective delivery of library media services and programs.

2. Update print and non-print materials to support the current curriculum and to meet Illinois standards.
3. Purchase software such as CD-ROMs and enable WWW access to enhance the students' school experiences.
4. Automate card catalog and circulation system.
5. Update audiovisual equipment and house appropriately.
6. Acquire appropriate equipment for students with special needs.
7. Integrate the library technology services throughout all areas of the curriculum.
8. Install new computer furniture.
9. Limit the number of study hall students when classes are scheduled in the library.

Memorial Junior/Senior High School Library Media Center Program

- Vision

The Bennet Grove Public Schools Library Media Program provides all students with a viable library media program integrated with the curriculum. With the cooperation of the staff the library media program will enable students to find, evaluate, and use information. As a result of the library media program the students will become independent, productive, lifelong learners who will enhance and contribute to the community.

- Mission

The Bennet Grove Public Schools Library Media Program will enable students to become independent learners by stimulating a love of reading and learning.

- Program Goals

Learning and Teaching:
- Collaborate with teachers to design learning strategies that foster information problem solving, and meet the individual learning styles, abilities, and needs of students.
- Integrate information problem solving strategies and electronic resources throughout the curriculum.

Information Access and Delivery:
- Provide intellectual and physical access to print and electronic resources in a variety of formats.
- Collaborate with other educational and library organizations.
- Provide an atmosphere that encourages the development of lifelong learners.

Program Administration:
- Provide a program that functions as the information center of the school.
- Provide a facility, staff, and budget appropriate for implementing the vision and mission of the program.
- Provide electronic resources and up-to-date policies for access and use of the library media center.
- Communicate and advocate for an exemplary library media program.

Action Plan Goals, Objectives, and Activities

Goal 1: Provide adequate resources and staff to support the curriculum at Bennet Grove Memorial Junior/Senior High School.

Objectives:

    1.1   Identify the staffing needs of the library media center to provide adequate levels of professional staff to ensure the effective delivery of library media services and programs.

    1.2   Update print and electronic resources to support the current Bennet Grove curriculum and to meet the resource needs of the Illinois Curriculum guidelines.

    1.3   Organize a Library Media Center Advisory Team to assist in the development of the resources of the Library Media Center.

Activity	Description	Timeline	Responsibility	Resources	Measure
1.1.1	Based on the accreditors recommendation, the new staffing pattern of one library media specialist and one assistant librarian will be maintained	October budget	Library media specialist, principal, superintendent	Student enrollment projections	Continued funding of one library media specialist and one assistant librarian.
1.2.1	Analyze local and Illinois curriculum as they relate to teaching and learning in Bennet Grove.	Spring 2000 ongoing through fall 2001	As curricula are established and accepted by school committee, library media specialist will work with dept. heads to develop list of resource needs current and projected for print and electronic resources.	Accepted curriculum guides	Resources in the library media center to support curricula needs
1.2.2	Based on curricula needs organize a collection development plan for the systematic acquisition of materials (print and electronic resources) over a three year period	Develop a collection development plan in conjunction with curricula needs in spring 2000 through fall 2001	Library media specialist, curriculum department heads, teachers, principal, curriculum coordinator	Needs and projected needs (collection development plan) (print and electronic resources) to support curricula along with cost projections	Completed plan for purchasing
1.2.3	Evaluate the collection against curricula needs to determine its relevancy.	Spring 2000 to spring 2001	Library media specialist, teachers, curricula dept. heads	Curricula frameworks	Weeded collection, which reflects curricula needs of the school.
1.2.4	Work with . . . to acquire the free online databases available to libraries	Spring 2000	Library media specialist, public librarian, network coordinator	Materials available from state agencies, public library, etc.	Databases being used in the library media center.
1.2.5	Review other on-line databases to determine which would best supplement resources from other agencies, e.g., state, regional, public library	Fall 2000	Library media specialist	Conference attendance, visit other high school LMCs, read reviews in professional journals.	Databases being used in the library media center.

Activity	Description	Timeline	Responsibility	Resources	Measure
1.2.6	Meet with teachers by dept. to discuss new resources, requested resources, research topics, and integration of information problem solving	Fall 2001	Library media specialist, curriculum dept. heads	Bibliographic lists	Written feedback from teachers
1.2.7	Prepare for adequate site licenses to enable all identified electronic resources to be used on expanded library computer network of computers.	Fall 2000	Library media specialist, principal, network coordinator	Budget	On-line resources available in the new library media center.
1.2.8	Establish access Establish access to WWW; evaluate the purchase of a server for CD-ROM access from the new LMC to the classrooms.	Fall 2000	Library media specialist, principal, network coordinator	Evaluation of available servers from professional sources	CD-ROMs available for use; WWW-based services, etc.
1.3.1	Organize the LMC Advisory Team. Invite participation by the principal or his/her designee and by a representative teacher from each grade in the school.	Fall 2000	Library media specialist, principal	None	Library Media Center Advisory Team in place

Goal 2: Provide on-line electronic access to the materials in the library media center and beyond.

Objectives:

2.1   Identify the automation system to convert the card catalog and circulation system.

2.2   Prepare the library media center for conversion to an automated on-line card catalog and circulation system.

2.3   Provide access to well-reviewed Internet sites integrated with the curriculum through the on-line catalog.

Activity	Description	Timeline	Responsibility	Resources	Measure
2.1.1	Evaluate automation system being used by the Bennet Grove Public Library	Spring 2000	Library media specialist	None	Notes from meeting
2.1.2	Establish criteria for school's evaluation of automation systems; identify three automation systems that meet these best and compare them.	Spring 2000 to fall 2000	Library media specialist, technology coordinator, network coordinator, principal, curriculum coordinator, Library Media Center Advisory Team	Professional journals, Internet, Professional books, develop comparison matrix, visits to library media centers that have the three automation systems, presentations by leading automation system representatives, budget support	Automation system in place
2.2.1	Weed the collection in preparation for automation	Spring 2000 to fall 2000	Library media specialist, curriculum dept. heads, teachers, Library Media Center Advisory Team	Curriculum documents	Up-to-date collection in place
2.2.2	Retrospective conversion: automate existing collection for use with on-line catalog and circulation system	Fall 2000 to spring 2001	Library media specialist, technology coordinator, network coordinator, principal	Company to do the conversion, budget support	Whole collection on-line
2.3.1	Work with automation company to select appropriate Internet sites for access through the on-line catalog	Spring 2001	Library media specialist, curriculum dept. heads, teachers curriculum coordinator, technology coordinator, Library Media Center Advisory Team	Professional resources	Access to appropriate curriculum related Internet sites available through the on-line catalog.

114

Goal 3: Provide intellectual and physical assess to the resources of the library media center, print and electronic.

Objectives:

3.1 Develop a 9–12 information problem-solving curriculum that will be integrated into the 9–12 curriculum of the school.

3.2 Encourage collaboration and joint planning between the classroom teachers and the Library Media Specialist.

3.3 Improve the teaching learning process by developing technology and information problem–solving workshops for the teachers.

Activity	Description	Timeline	Responsibility	Resources	Measure
3.1.1	Develop a 9–12 curriculum based on an information problem-solving model along with basic print and electronic media competencies. It would also include ethical issues.	Begin in fall 2000 through fall 2001	Library media specialist, Library Media Center Advisory Team, curriculum dept. heads, curriculum coordinator	9–12 curriculum guides, resources available through the library media center	Completed curriculum guide for information problem solving
3.2.1	Invite teachers to use the library media center and the collaborative planning and teaching services of the library media specialist	Spring 2000	Library media specialist, teachers, curriculum dept. heads	Print and electronic resources	Library media specialist plan book, display with projects students completed as a result of joint planning and teaching.
3.3.1	Work with the curriculum coordinator to run professional development workshops for teachers to teach them how to access, use, and evaluate the new electronic resources and the new information problem-solving model.	Begin planning in spring 2001 for implementation in fall 2001	Library media specialist, curriculum coordinator, Library Media Center Advisory Team	Access to electronic resources	Workshops will have been held

Goal 4: Assist new teachers in integrating information literacy standards into the curriculum.

Objective:

4.1 Ensure that teachers and students are efficient and effective users and producers of information.

Activity	Description	Timeline	Responsibility	Resources	Measure
4.1.1	Meet with new teachers and discuss the library media center programs and policies. Discuss the integration of information problem solving into the curriculum to improve student use of information.	September 2000	Library media specialist	Policies and library resources	Effective use of the library media center by the new faculty members
4.1.2	With new teachers, identify areas of curriculum for initial collaboration.	September 2000	Library media specialist, new teachers, dept. heads	Curriculum guidelines	Successful initial collaboration

Goal 5: Provide, as needed, appropriate assistive/adaptive technology for students with special needs.

Objectives:

5.1   Work with the special needs coordinator and the guidance counselors to open the lines of communication relative to any assistive/adaptive technology needs of students as identified in IEPs.

5.2   Develop budget related to purchasing needed assistive/adaptive technology for special needs students.

5.3   Ensure access for all in the new library media facility.

Activity	Description	Timeline	Responsibility	Resources	Measure
5.1.1	Send a memo to the special needs coordinator and the guidance counselors informing them of the need of the library media center to participate in responding to Student adaptive/technology needs as identified in IEPs.	Every spring	Library media specialist, special needs coordinator, guidance counselors, school nurse	IEPs	As needed, Adaptive/ assistive technology in place in the library media center.
5.2.1	Develop a budget, as needed, for assistive/adaptive technology	Yearly, as needed	Library media specialist, special needs coordinator, guidance counselors, school nurse	Catalogs, appropriate vendors	Adaptive/ assistive technology in place in the library media center.
5.2.2	Purchase assistive/ adaptive technology as identified.	Yearly, as needed	Library media specialist, special needs coordinator, guidance counselors, school	None needed	Adaptive/ assistive technology in place in the library media center.

Activity	Description	Timeline	Responsibility	Resources	Measure
			nurse		
5.3.1	Review and make changes as need in the placement of bookcases, tables, computer desk, etc. to ensure ADA compatibility	Spring 2000 to fall 2000	Principal, school building committee, superintendent, school committee	If You Build It, Will They Come? ALA Publication, 2000	New facility is ADA compli-ant.

Goal 6: Provide adequate and equitable access to all of the information resources: print and electronic available through the library media center for information problem solving, addressing curricula issues, and personal interest s in pursuit of learning skills to be used for a life time.

Objective:

6.1   Review existing policies and update or create new ones to meet the current needs.

Activity	Description	Timeline	Responsibility	Resources	Measure
6.1.1	Review and update the following policies: book selection, acceptable use, circulation, behavior, lost, damaged, and overdue books	Fall 2000	Library media specialist, library media advisory team, principal, school committee	Current policies	Updated policies available and in use.

Goal 7: Provide an orderly transition of the library media facility in the move to the new high school building.

Objective:

7.1 Put together a plan of what needs to be moved, how it will be moved, and where it will go in the new facility.

Activity	Description	Timeline	Responsibility	Resources	Measure
7.1.1	Plan the details of the move of the library resources, etc.	March 2001	Library Media Specialist, Principal, Director of Maintenance, Custodial Staff, Volunteers	None needed	A plan in place
7.1.2	Facilitate the orderly moving of the library resources, etc.	Summer 2001	Library Media, Specialist, Principal, Director of Maintenance, Custodial Staff, Volunteers	Boxes, tape, dolly, packing labels, bubble wrap, time	A successful move

REFERENCES

Adcock, Donald, ed. (2000). *A planning guide for Information Power: Building partnerships for learning with School Library Media Program assessment rubric for the 21st century.* Chicago, IL: American Association of School Librarians.

Bradford, Robert W., et al (1999). *Simplified strategic planning: A no-nonsense guide for busy people who want results fast.* Worcester, MA: Chandler House Press.

Fontana, A. & Frey, J. H. (1994). *Interviewing: The art of science.* In N. K. Denzin & Y. S. Lincoln (Eds.), Handbook of qualitative research (p. 361–376). Thousand Oaks, CA: Sage.

Himmel, E. & Wilson, W. J. (1998). *Planning for results: A public library transformation process.* Chicago, IL: American Library Association.

Information power: Building partnerships for learning. (1998). Chicago, IL: American Library Association.

Keegan, B. & Westerberg, T. (1991). "Restructuring and the School Library: Partners in an Information Age." *NASSP Bulletin*: 9–14.

Lance, K. C., Welborn, L., & Hamilton-Pennell, C. (1993). *The impact of school library media centers on academic achievement.* Castle Rock, CO: Hi Willow Research.

LeBaron, J. & Markuson, C. (1991). "Planning: A necessary anchor for the school media program." *Wilson Library Bulletin.* 42–45, 132.

Loertscher. D. V. (1988). *Taxonomies of the school library media program.* Englewood, CO: Libraries Unlimited

National Educational Technology Standards for Students. (1998). Eugene, OR: International Society for Technology in Education.

NEEMA "Task Force to Develop Competencies, Questions for Evaluators, and Indicators of Quality for the School Library Media Program." (1998, June). *Final report.* Unpublished manuscript.

Questionnaire Standards for accreditation: Library technology and media services. (1998). New England Association of Schools and Colleges, Commission on Public Secondary Schools. Burlington, MA: New England Association of Schools and Colleges.

Rea, L. M. & Parker, R. A. (1992). *Designing and conducting survey research.* San Francisco, CA: Jossey Bass.

Rubin, R. J. (1992). *The Planning process for Massachusetts' prison libraries: A workbook designed for the Massachusetts Department of Correction.* Boston, MA: Massachusetts Board of Library Commissioners.

Shannon, M. & Baker, B. (1990). *The Small libraries planning process: A planning workbook for public library development in Massachusetts.* Boston, MA: Massachusetts Board of Library Commissioners.

Standards for school library media centers in the Commonwealth of Massachusetts. [1997]. MA: Massachusetts School Library Media Association.

Weaver, B. & Markuson, C. (1995). *Competencies for prospective teachers and administrators.* Chicago, IL: American Association of School Librarians.

Wiggins, G. & McTighe, J. (1998, March). *Understanding by Design.* Paper presented at the meeting of the Association for Supervision and Curriculum Development, San Antonio, TX.

ABOUT THE AUTHORS

Mary Frances Zilonis, Ed.D., is director of information technology at Newton Public Schools in Lakewood, Massachusetts. Prior to that she was professor of instructional technology and library science at Bridgewater State College, where she also served as chair of the Secondary Education and Professional Programs Department. She holds a doctorate in educational media and technology from Boston University.

Carolyn Markuson, Ed.D., is an educational program consultant who specializes in the areas of media and technology, instructional design skills, facilities design, and library and information programs. She is president and founder of biblioTECH Corporation and has designed over eighty new and renovated school libraries.

Mary Beth Fincke has served as the associate director of EDCO School Services (Educational Collaborative of Greater Boston), which provides grant writing and collaborative educational and professional development services to its members. Now living on Cape Cod, Ms. Fincke gives back to the community by volunteering in local school and public libraries and other charitable activities.

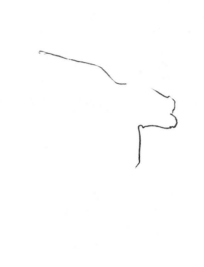